The Painted Voyage

Michael Jacobs

The Painted Voyage

Art, Travel and Exploration 1564-1875

Published for the Trustees of the British Museum
by British Museum Press

FOR PAUL STIRTON, 'FELLOW ART TRAVELLER'

© 1995 The Trustees of the British Museum

Published by British Museum Press
A division of The British Museum Company Ltd
46 Bloomsbury Street
London WC1B 3QQ

The right of Michael Jacobs to be identified
as the author of this Work
has been asserted in accordance with the
Copyright, Designs and Patent Act 1988.

British Library Cataloguing in Publication Data
A catalogue record for this book is available
from the British Library

ISBN 0 7141 1656 4

Designed by Alan Bartram
Typeset in Baskerville by Rowland Phototypesetting Ltd,
Bury St Edmunds, Suffolk
Printed in Spain

FRONTISPIECE
Thomas and William Daniell
viewing Bijaigarh from the south-west
(detail), by William Daniell

ACKNOWLEDGEMENTS

For advice about the Orientalists I am grateful to Caroline Juler
and Brian MacDermot, Director of the Mathaf Gallery; Jocelyn
Hackforth-Jones was generous with her expertise on Augustus
Earle and Australian art, while Fintan Cullen, Paul Stirton,
Matilde Mateo Sevilla and Janie Munro were helpful on a variety
of other matters. I must also thank the staff of the India House
Library, the British Library Map Room and Manuscript
Department, the Museum of Mankind and the British Museum
Print Room, in particular Antony Griffiths. Not least, I must
acknowledge a great debt to the writings on India, the South
Pacific and America by Mildred Archer, Bernard Smith and
Hugh Honour respectively. The idea for this book was proposed
to me by Rachel Rogers, formerly of British Museum Press. My
thanks to her and to the rest of the staff there, especially Julie
Young and my patient and conscientious editor, Joanna
Champness. Jackie's support, once again, goes without saying.

Contents

John White, *Map of Eastern North America: Florida to Chesapeake Bay*, 1850s; pen and watercolour, British Museum. More decorative than useful, this map features long stretches of the American coast that had yet to be surveyed by the English. For Florida, White had to rely heavily on the work of his great French predecessor, Le Moyne.

R G V

Chesepiuc.
O.
Scicoac.

Weapemeoc.

Chawanoc.   Maquetuc.   Croatamung.

Moratuc.   Etacrewaci.
Tramaskecooc.   Port Ferdinando.
                                 Hatorask.
Secotan   Aquascacooc.

I A

Pasquip.
Pomeiooc. Mentō.   Paquiac.

R S
                              Dasomonpeuc. Croatoan.

CIGATEO.

IANE   GVANIMA.
           Scicoac.

4A   J

39

38   G

37

36

35

34

33

32

31

30

29

28

27

26

25

Thomas Ender, *Concert on Board the Frigate Austria*, 1817; pencil and wash, Akademie der bildenden Künste, Vienna. The Viennese artist Thomas Ender formed part of a team of scientists who travelled to Brazil on the same boat that carried the Archduchess Leopoldina of Austria to her future husband, Don Pedro of Brazil. The concert shown here was one of the various entertainments intended to make the long crossing to Rio more bearable.

Introduction

Art has played no less a role than literature in promoting fanciful western notions of distant lands. But words preceded pictures in the creation of this mythology, perhaps because words, by leaving more to the imagination, were better suited to evoke the extreme fantasy of the earliest visions of faraway places.

The person who did most to inspire an early interest in the exotic was the Venetian merchant Marco Polo, who was claimed in the prologue to his famous book of travels to have journeyed more extensively than any man since the Creation. Recent evidence suggests that Polo's book might have been a hoax which relied heavily on descriptions by earlier travellers such as Ibn-Battuta. The truthfulness of Polo's account is ultimately perhaps of little importance, for fact and fiction have always coexisted in the perception of foreign lands. Long after the Middle Ages, when such fabled domains as Cathay and the Land of Prester John had disappeared from western consciousness, visions no less illusory were conjured up instead. Places that are imagined have sometimes a greater presence than those that are real, as the cynical Portuguese writer Fernando Pessoa acknowledged. 'Travel books', he wrote, 'are . . . worth only as much as the imagination of the one who writes them. And if the one who writes them has imagination, he can enchant us with the detailed, photographic description of landscapes he's imagined just as well as with the necessarily less detailed description of the landscapes he thought he saw.'

Most of the more adventurous artist travellers, from the earliest Renaissance ones right up to those of the mid nineteenth century, travelled as members of diplomatic or scientific missions, and had to assume responsibilities that appeared to leave little room for artistic licence: they were employed to make an objective record of the peoples, landscapes, animals, flora and fauna of the countries they visited or explored. Yet despite this brief, and despite the insistence of so many of them on the scientific accuracy of their work, their visions of foreign lands were inevitably influenced by their western prejudices and preconceptions, by the demands of colonial propaganda, and by the need to create finished pictures that would not only entertain and inform but also be composed according to the artistic conventions of the time. The viewer of their pictures must also bear in mind that many of the more memorable finished ones were done on the artists' return to their home countries and are thus further distorted by memory. 'In being filtered through memory', wrote the French orientalist painter and writer Fromentin, 'truth becomes a poem and landscape a picture.'

For much of history the travelling artist in exotic lands has been thought of essentially as a draughtsman or illustrator rather than as a practitioner of high art.

Furthermore, many of those contracted to accompany expeditions were obliged also to take on menial jobs; John White, for instance, was made to work as purser when he journeyed with Sir Richard Grenville to Virginia in 1578. Even as late as 1858, when Romanticism had given a new importance to pictures of exotic places, the artist travelling with Livingstone to the Zambezi had the additional job of 'store-keeper'.

The origins of the travelling artist are especially modest, and date back to the fifteenth century, when sketches executed on sea journeys helped to supplement nautical records. The works by John White, which are among the earliest original drawings to survive of any distant land, were probably no more highly regarded as works of art than were these navigational tools: they were scientific illustrations which, when engraved by De Bry, had also a great popular appeal, substantiating travellers' tales of the fabled New World.

Though travelling artists were a prerequisite of all scientific and diplomatic missions from the sixteenth century onwards, they found themselves particularly in demand in the eighteenth century, thanks to the so-called virtuosi and their empirical and encyclopaedic curiosity in the world. Newly-founded institutions, such as Britain's Society of Dilettanti and the Society of Arts, sent artists and scientists to observe little-known parts of the world, and to record the wealth of archaeological sites that started coming to light, especially those on the shores of the Mediterranean. The idea of travel as an activity that broadened the mind led young aristocrats and gentlemen to spend long periods abroad, usually in France or Italy, and often in the company of an artist or even a scientist; the more adventurous of them went beyond the conventional countries of the Grand Tour and visited such places as Spain, North Africa and the Near East. Towards the end of the eighteenth century, Captain Cook established a particularly exotic alternative to the Grand Tour by equipping his Pacific expeditions with teams of artists and gentleman scholars.

William Hodges, who accompanied Cook on the second of these journeys, was one of the first artists on a scientific expedition to go beyond mere topographical draughtsmanship and transform his illustrations of exotic places into works of art. Had he worked in the Mediterranean he might have been taken seriously as an artist, but the fact that he painted Pacific scenes meant that this could never be possible, despite the concessions he made in his finished pictures to classical conventions. Hodges, in a reversal of the story of Gauguin, was eventually forced by dwindling fortunes to turn from painting the tropics to banking.

Well into the nineteenth century, the European vision of Nature continued to be influenced by such artistic concepts as the Picturesque and the Sublime, and by notions of an Italianate ideal as represented by the paintings of Claude Lorraine and Salvator Rosa. Meanwhile, the indigenous, semi-naked peoples of distant lands were invariably imagined in terms not just of the 'noble savage' but also of the ancient Greeks and Romans. Similarly strong expectations affected those hundreds of artists who, in the early nineteenth century, were lured to the Orient, where they hoped to encounter scenes of violent passion and steamy sensuality. Wherever they travelled, artists reinforced stereotypical images of the exotic, and in so doing furthered romantic visions that were likely to lead to disappointment among those

William Alexander, *The Chinese Ambassador Receiving Lord Macartney's Embassy, 14 September 1793*; pen and wash, the British Library Oriental and India Office Collections. Lord Macartney travelled to Peking in 1793 in the hope of persuading the Chinese to open up their country to western trade. Though he failed in this, his embassy did at least provide – thanks to the accompanying artist William Alexander – the finest and most extensive of the early pictorial records of inland China.

who later visited the countries in question. 'A common source of disappointment to travellers', wrote a contributor to the 1869 issue of *Illustrated Travels*, 'is their unreasonable expectation of finding a country peopled with painters' models. Nowhere are they so likely to be so disappointed as in Spain; for of no country in Europe are the preconceptions in the minds of foreigners to so great an extent based upon the labours of the artist.'

By the mid-nineteenth century a more scientific attitude towards the representation of Nature had undoubtedly developed among artists, prompted by critics such as Ruskin, and, above all, by the explorer and naturalist Alexander Humboldt, who encouraged landscape artists to turn away from Europe and to find beauty in the Tropics, where Nature was at her most extreme. Yet at the same time the spirit of the Romantic movement made artists more subjective in their approach towards Nature, and led them to impose their own emotions on the landscapes they depicted. A new type of travelling artist emerged – one who journeyed on his own, impelled by a romantic restlessness. 'We are destined to die young,' wrote the French Orientalist painter Henri Regnault, 'we lead too itinerant a life.'

Many of the earlier travelling artists, such as William Hodges, had been encouraged by their first taste of exotic travel to continue afterwards to other exotic

locations. However, none of these artists travelled quite so extensively or obsessively as some of the independent ones of the nineteenth century. Someone who fulfilled Regnault's prediction of an early death was Augustus Earle, whose 'roving disposition', according to *Bryan's Dictionary of Painters and Engravers*, led to his being called '"the wandering artist"'. 'He had', runs his entry in *Bryan's Dictionary*,

roamed in Africa – rambled in the United States – sketched in South America – attempted to go to the Cape of Good Hope in a worn-out Margate hoy . . . visited . . . New Zealand, where he drew from the naked figure, and saw the finest forms of the world, addicted to cannibalism . . . by way of variety, proceeded to the Caroline Islands – stopped at the Ladrones – looked in upon Manilla, and finally settled himself at Madras, and made money as a portrait painter. Not content, he went to Pondicherry and there embarked for France, but stopped at Mauritius, and after some few more calls at various places, found his way home.

No less restless, if slightly more limited in the geographical scope of his travels, was the English artist and humorist Edward Lear, who, in a letter of 1880 to his American publisher, James Fields, summarised the philosophy of the nineteenth-century artist traveller. 'The painter', he wrote, 'who all his life paints Surrey woodlands or English coast scenes arrives at a perfection in what he aims at, and is a

Augustus Earle, *View from the Summit of the Cacavada [Corcovado] Mountains, near Rio,* 1821-4; watercolour, Rex Nan Kivell Collection, National Library of Australia, Canberra. The artist, in his top hat, registers wonder at the sight of the bay of Rio with its famous Sugar Loaf rock.

delight and benefactor – but he who can portray Arctic scenes, South American magnificences and endless other distinctly various phases of nature, is far more a delight and a far greater benefactor to his art and country.'

The painter who Lear had in mind was the American Frederic Church, a copy of whose *The Heart of the Andes* (see pages 138-9) hung by his bedside in his later years. By transforming the results of intense on-the-spot observation into a sublime and largely imaginary whole, Church represented in his works the ultimate to which the intrepid artist could now aspire. It is also with Church and his American contemporaries that journeys to far-away places came finally to be regarded, in America at least, as being as beneficial to an artist's development as a stay in Italy or Paris. In 1859, the year when *The Heart of the Andes* was exhibited, an article in the *Cosmopolitan Art Journal* stated that

Artists are now scattered, like leaves or thistle blossoms, over the whole face of the country, in pursuit of their annual study of nature and necessary recreation. Some have gone far toward the North Pole, to invade the haunts of the iceberg with their inquisitive and unsparing eye – some have gone to the far West, where Nature plays with the illimitable and grand – some have become tropically mad, and are pursuing a sketch up and down the Cordilleras, through Central America and down the Andes.

The wealth of source material relating to the travels of nineteenth-century artists testifies to the particular difficulties and dangers they faced when working in exotic locations. Apart from such general worries and discomforts as disease, insects and brigand attacks, artists who sketched ran the danger of offending local customs and, above all, of being mistaken as spies: 'the idea of political espionage is ever associated with the act of topographical drawing', wrote Lear, echoing the view of the Spanish traveller Richard Ford that 'nothing gave greater suspicion than a foreigner making sketches'.

The working methods of most of the intrepid artists up to the mid-nineteenth century reflected these difficult conditions. Pressure of time forced the majority to execute quick sketches in pencil, ink or watercolour; few of them had the leisure to paint outdoors in oils, which in any case were liable to melt from the heat of the sun. Lear, who rarely spent as much as an hour or two in any of the thousands of spots he sketched, wrote that 'Even let the landscape be ever so tempting, the uncertainty of meeting with any place of repose or shelter obliges the most enthusiastic artist to pass hastily through scenes equal or superior to any it may be again his lot to see.'

The rapidly assembled material executed abroad was often put into a more finished state during the long, tedious periods of quarantine generally enforced upon exotic travellers disembarking at a French port. The sketches, supplemented sometimes by a wide range of souvenirs, from clothing to live animals, were used on the artist's return home as the basis of academy pictures, panoramas (a popular attraction of the late eighteenth and early nineteenth centuries), and especially prints to accompany scientific works or illustrated books of travels. Many artists relied on the proceeds of such works to fund future trips; others managed to extract from a single journey enough material to last them for the rest of their lives. A number of professionals who had worked in exotic lands derived additional income

George Catlin, *Stalking Buffalo*, from *Souvenir of the American Indians*, vol. 2; pencil, Museum of Mankind, London. 'The author and his faithful Indian guide approaching a numerous herd on a level prairie, under masques of the white wolf skin', runs the artist's own caption to this drawing. He can clearly be seen on the right-hand side, sketching under conditions which are perhaps unique in the history of art.

from being asked to improve upon and make fit for publication the countless sketches brought back from abroad by intrepid amateurs, in particular women travellers, such as Florence Nightingale's close friend Selina Bracebridge, whose numerous drawings of the Middle East were used by David Roberts and others for an illustrated edition of the Bible.

The role of the artist as a recorder of distant lands was seriously threatened with the invention of the daguerreotype in 1833. Though travelling artists, such as the Daniells, had occasionally relied on camera obscuras, the daguerreotype promised a speed and accuracy in topographical representation that the human hand could not match. 'Daguerre is my Chimborazo', pronounced Humboldt in reference to the Ecuadorian volcano that had established his credentials both as a scientist and an adventurer. Camera equipment, and the laboratory of chemicals that went with it, proved at first too cumbersome to be taken on difficult journeys; but the experience of travelling was to be altered radically after Kodak had brought out the first portable camera in 1888.

With the invention of the camera, the whole issue of truthfulness in the portrayal of places would seem to be resolved. Yet, right from the very early days of photography, there were those who insisted that the camera also could lie, and that the beauty of nature could only truly be captured through the subjective vision of an artist. The Orientalist painter and writer Eugène Fromentin, though one of the many travelling artists of the late nineteenth century to use photographs as the basis of his finished works, was only too aware of the limitations of this medium. '[Photographs]', he pronounced after a visit to North Africa in 1870, 'give you only a partial idea of the beauty of things; you will not find in them either the incomparable quality of light, nor the sense of scale . . . nor the special colour of the Sahara, which contains the subtlest hues of black.'

1

The World of the Orientalist

Wenceslas Hollar, *Tangier*, 1688; watercolour, British Museum. The Moroccan port of Tangier, a British possession at the time of Hollar's visit, is given here a remarkably European look.

'That is a memorable day to the artist when he first exchanges the north of Europe for an Eastern clime', wrote John Seddon in 1858, describing how his artist brother Thomas fell immediately and – as it turned out – fatally under the spell of the Orient.

The Orient, a term evoking lands more imaginary than real, embraces a vast and indeterminate area stretching from Tangier to Tokyo. However, to the many artists

who came to specialise in 'oriental' scenes in the nineteenth century, the 'Orient'
meant essentially those Islamic lands bordering on the Mediterranean: Morocco,
Algeria, and the countries falling within the enormous Ottoman Empire, including
Tunisia, Egypt, the Holy Land, Syria, Lebanon, and Cyprus. A number of the
'Orientalists' found a foretaste of this Orient in both Spain and the Balkans, while
others derived 'oriental' inspiration even from Poland and Hungary. Only the most
intrepid artists made it as far as Arabia and Persia. The 'Orient', as understood by
the majority of European artists, represented an exotic destination far closer to home
than any other of the distant lands that fired romantic imaginations.

Western interest in the Orient grew in tandem with the declining threat of Islam
to the West. European geographers and other academics began seriously to study
North Africa and the Near East from the early sixteenth century onwards, when the
West had come to dominate the Mediterranean trade routes, and Islam had lost its
last foothold in Spain; but it was with Turkey's diminished power in Europe after the

Treaty of Karlowitz in 1699, and the consequent waning of its empire in the eighteenth and nineteenth centuries, that western scholarship and travel literature on the Orient proliferated as never before.

Written records of the Orient at first greatly outnumbered the pictorial ones, and only a handful of topographical artists are known to have worked in the Islamic world before 1700. Of the professionals the most prolific was the Dutchman Cornelius de Brujn, who provided the first detailed pictorial record of Persia and the Levant. Another artist was the famous Bohemian-born engraver Wenceslas Hollar, who spent twelve months in Tangier in 1668, and was almost killed by pirates on the way back.

Tangier, at the time of Hollar's visit, was a British colony, acquired six years earlier as part of the marriage dowry from Catherine of Braganza to Charles II. Hollar had gone there on a mission led by the Earl of Arundel's grandson, Henry Howard, to report on the precarious state of a colony that would eventually be abandoned in 1684, after the expenditure of a vast amount of the court's money. Charles II, who had thought of Tangier as a 'jewell of immense value in the royal diadem', saw the colony as a base for grander colonial designs on Africa, and had been tempted by Hollar's offer to 'give account to his Majestie . . . of all what is worthy to be observed in those parts, especially the Citty of Tangier'.

As is the case generally with art and exotic travel, the artistic depiction of the Orient, from the time of Hollar until the mid-nineteenth century, was closely connected with western policies of colonial expansion. The great majority of the early 'Orientalists' were from France or Britain, the two countries with the greatest stake in North Africa and the Near East during this period. France acquired Algeria in 1830, and acted as advisers and instructors to the Ottoman army until superseded by Germany in the late nineteenth century. After the failure of Britain's involvement in Tangier, British interests in the Orient were concentrated on Egypt and the Near East, which occupied a vital strategic position on the trade route with India. It was primarily to weaken the British that Napoleon undertook his disastrous Egyptian campaign of 1798-1801.

Of the many artists who visited the Orient as members of diplomatic missions or military expeditions, the largest group were those who accompanied Napoleon to Egypt as part of the famous 'Commission des sciences et des arts de l'armée de l'orient'. This team of 167 scholars and artists, known collectively as the 'Savants', set out to produce a systematic record of the lands Napoleon hoped to conquer, the emphasis of the artists being on Egypt's ancient monuments. The science of Egyptology was born.

The archaeological exploration of the Orient went hand in hand with colonial ambitions, and provided the main source of employment for most of the artists who visited these lands up to the 1850s. The eighteenth and early nineteenth centuries saw some of the most important discoveries and excavations in the history of the Near East. Baalbek and Palmyra were brought to light in the 1750s, and Petra in 1812; the ancient cities of Asia Minor were excavated from the mid-eighteenth century onwards, while archaeological work on Karnak, Abu Simbel and the other monuments of Pharaonic Egypt was begun in earnest at the beginning of the

nineteenth century; the Assyrian cities of Mesopotamia were uncovered in the 1840s. Artists were an obligatory feature of all these expeditions, and were also frequently employed by the growing number of aristocrats and gentlemen who were encouraged by these sites to visit the Orient for both pleasure and education. A journey to the Orient came to be seen as an extension of the Grand Tour, and was even regarded as an exotic alternative to it by the time of Disraeli, who reflected the more progressive travelling tastes of the 1830s by undertaking a journey from Southern Spain all the way to Constantinople. In the words of the French painter Théodore Chassériau, visiting North Africa in 1846, 'Rome is no longer in Rome'.

Greater accessibility to the Orient, and a vastly improved knowledge of its lands, did little to diminish the many western myths that had grown up about the place. Though travellers were no longer finding unicorns here, as Ludovico Varthema had done on a visit to Arabia in 1503, they invariably came with romantic preconceptions based on the visions of other westerners. Many of the artists visited the Orient repeatedly and at great length, but they portrayed the place little differently from someone such as Delacroix, who, like other Orientalists, had developed a long-lasting passion for the Islamic world on the basis of a single and relatively short stay in Morocco and Algeria. Some of the Orientalist painters, in particular the Italians, never left Europe at all, and in so doing emulated the example of two of the writers who had most influenced western attitudes towards the Orient – Victor Hugo and Heinrich Heine.

The Orient of the western imagination acquired a life of its own independent of the real place. The Romantic writer and critic Théophile Gautier, confronted by an Egyptian landscape by the pioneering Orientalist Prosper Marilhat, felt an immediate 'nostalgia for the Orient, where I have never set foot'. 'I believed', he continued, 'that I had discovered at last my true homeland, and, when I turned my eyes away from this vivid canvas, I experienced a sense of exile.' Marilhat's canvases had a comparable effect on the writer and painter Eugène Fromentin, who, like Gautier,

Jacques-Louis Denon, *The Artist Sketching in Upper Egypt*, *c.*1798; pen and wash, British Museum. The *Savants* who accompanied Napoleon to Egypt in 1798 included a large team of artists headed by Denon, who is here shown sketching whilst his Egyptian servant waits solicitously by with a seat.

William Müller, *The Great Harbour, Rhodes*, 1838; watercolour, British Museum. An artist of great freshness and spontaneity, Müller made his name with the watercolours he executed on a trip to Greece in 1838.

was inspired by them to visit the Orient himself. Once there, however, he was excited to find that 'the Orient, despite Marilhat . . . remains to be painted'. Unwittingly he went on to reveal the extent to which the Orient was not so much a geographical concept as an imaginary one that could be manipulated according to individual whims. 'I now have the right', he arrogantly wrote, 'to fashion the Orient in my own way and without imitating anyone.'

By the mid-nineteenth century artists travelling to the Orient had many well-established routes from which to choose. Those going to Constantinople, for instance, could take a boat down the Danube to the Black Sea, or sail directly from Southampton or Marseilles; with time to spare they could even travel through Italy, and feel the first pull of the Orient in Venice, which had been the traditional gateway to the East since the time of Marco Polo. 'The deep blue skies, and the still deeper blue waters of the lagunes', wrote the Victorian painter Frederick Goodall, 'gave me a foretaste of what I should see in Egypt.'

On the other side of the Atlantic the traveller reached the westernmost limits of the Ottoman Empire, which until 1820 embraced the whole of Greece, a country that had attracted surprisingly few visitors before the late eighteenth century. The

medieval and Renaissance fascination with ancient Greece did not extend to the modern country, which not only deterred travellers through being under the rule of the infidel, but also was imagined as some desolate impoverished wilderness bearing little relation to the Arcadian land featured in the work of its classical authors. Inevitably the ruins of Greece's classical past provided the main draw to the earliest travellers here; but it was not until as late as 1673-4 that an expedition of scholars carried out a study tour of the Aegean Islands. The expedition, led by the Marquis de Nontiel, included the artist Jacques Carrey, who became the first person to make detailed drawings of the pediments of the Parthenon.

A genuine Enlightenment interest in scholarship, combined with a desire for plundering or cheaply acquiring antiquities, inspired a dramatic growth of archaeological interest in Greece in the eighteenth and early nineteenth centuries, as it did throughout the Orient. By the beginning of the nineteenth century, Athens was witnessing a veritable invasion of European artists, the great majority of whom were uninspired architectural draughtsmen. 'They establish themselves in Athens for eight years', noted the Comte de Forbin in 1819, 'in order to draw three columns . . . and it is only after the efforts of many years that their sad watercolours reach the highest degree of boring perfection.'

William Müller, *Rock Tomb at Pinara*, 1843; watercolour, British Museum. Encouraged by the archaeologist Charles Fellows, Muller toured Lycia in south-west Turkey in 1842-3. By his own reckoning he made 'one or two hundred' drawings on this trip, of which many were of the celebrated ancient site of Pinara, where he spent nine days in the autumn of 1843.

However, by the time of Forbin's visit, an interest was at last growing in contemporary Greece, prompted by the social and political turmoil that would lead to the Greek War of Independence of 1820. The romantic espousal of the Greek cause by the likes of Byron was mirrored by the way in which artists began to portray the country's traditions and folklore, and to enliven their hitherto deserted architectural views with the addition of people in modern dress.

At the same time a strong appreciation of the Greek landscape was developing. In previous centuries the western vision of the classical world had not been able to accommodate the rocky barrenness of Greece, and had been based instead on the Arcadian lushness of Italy. Greek scenery now appealed to romantic tastes, and, what is more, corresponded to such an extent with the imagined landscapes of antiquity that the painter William Linton, in *The Scenery of Greece* (1856), could even state that 'Claude is often seen in Greece, and very rarely in Italy, though he never visited the former country.' According to Linton the ancient Greeks lived in a 'territory which was but a series of pictures', and the landscapes surrounding them 'had made them poets and artists from their cradles'.

For some of the Orientalists, such as Decamps and J.-F. Lewis, Greece may have lacked the excitement and colourful exoticism of the Near East; but to others it represented an unsurpassed harmonious integration between landscape and architecture. One of the first artists to portray the Greek environment evocatively and without pedantry was the remarkable if short-lived Bristol painter, William Müller, whose visit to Greece in 1838 was a prelude to trips to Egypt and Asia Minor. But perhaps the greatest and certainly the most prolific painter of the Greek landscape was Edward Lear, who loved Greece more than any other of the Mediterranean countries that he devoted so much of his life to recording.

Few artists deserve the epithet of 'artist traveller' as much as Lear; from the time of his first visit to continental Europe in 1837 up to his death in 1888 he was rarely to spend more than a few months in any one place. His restlessness stemmed from a passionate love of the new and from an obsession with amassing a vast portfolio of topographical sketches; but it was also his way of escaping from the problems of a life beset by depressive illness, epilepsy, financial worries, perpetual bachelorhood, and enormous complexes about both his looks and his lack of recognition as a serious artist.

When still in his early twenties Lear had gained a reputation as one of the outstanding ornithological draughtsmen of his age; and he would later achieve exceptional popularity for his nonsense verse, for which he is perhaps most widely known today. But it was in his desire to be recognised primarily as a landscape painter in oils that he was to experience endless frustration. His decision to turn to landscape only came when he was twenty-five; and it was not until twelve years later, after enrolling at the Royal Academy Schools in 1850, that he received any formal training as an artist. His attempts to be thought of as more than a mere topographical draughtsman would never be wholly fulfilled, and, furthermore, were belied by his belief in the drudgery of painting, his obvious preference for drawing, and by his often philistine attitude towards the old masters.

Lear's position as a traveller was similarly contradictory. On the one hand he had all the credentials of the true traveller, having far greater stamina and will-power than most people, while also believing that travel was an activity best undertaken on one's own rather than in the company of diplomats, soldiers or academics. Yet in many other ways Lear was the least intrepid of artists. 'Nothing daunted him', wrote Holman Hunt, 'and yet no-one could be more fearful than he of certain difficulties he had to face as the fixed condition of travelling.' Wary of noise and confusion, delicate in constitution, incapable of violence even in self-defence, and terrified of dogs, horses, revolutionaries, customs officials and sea journeys, Lear seems at times to have been kept going purely through his remarkable sense of humour, his puritanical discipline, and through an absorption in his work which could make him write that 'the wayfarer soon forgets the inconveniences of travel while recording with pen and pencil its excitement and interests'.

As with Frederick Goodall and so many other artists of the time, Lear had his introduction to the Mediterranean world in Italy; but it is a measure of his adventurousness and originality that he went beyond the well-trodden Italian sites and explored more inaccessible and lesser-known areas such as the Abruzzi and Calabria. A comparable thoroughness was to characterise his many journeys around Greece, which he finally reached in 1848, over ten years after his first visit to Italy. His Grecian travels began conventionally enough in Corfu (a Turkish possession until 1864), which was already so popular with the British that all the donkeys available for hire were usually appropriated for picnic parties; but later he became apparently the first Englishman to visit the promontory of Akrokeramos, where he 'lived on rugs and ate with gipsies and unclean persons and performed frightful discrepancies for eight days'. His curiosity also took him to the remote and exotic-seeming Mount Athos, which was divested by him of some of its mystique in his witty descriptions of the 'muttering, miserable, mutton-hating, man-avoiding, misogynic, morose and merriment-marring, monotoning, many-mule-making, mournful, minced-fish and marmalade-masticating Monx'.

On his way to and from Greece and the Near East, Lear also braved a few times the route through Islamic Albania, a country as dangerous and little known then as it is now. Here he experienced the difficulties that many artists have had to face in Islamic countries, where religion forbids the representation of figurative subjects. On at least three occasions, while sketching, he was pelted with stones and taunted with shouts of '*Shatan*' or 'Devil!' The first time this happened, at Monastir, the local pasha had to protect him with a bodyguard armed with a whip; at Ochrid he tried to protect himself by donning a fez; and at Elbassa, when bystanders had begun screaming '*Shatan*' the moment they realised he was drawing their houses, he resorted to roaring with laughter, which soon had them laughing as well until told off for doing so by a ferocious dervish in a green turban.

Lear's interest in the Mediterranean was concentrated entirely on its eastern shores, and he never visited Spain, which rivalled Greece as a popular point of departure for the Orient. Whereas the East began in Venice, until comparatively recent times Africa was said to begin in Spain, of which Voltaire wrote in 1760 that it was 'a country we know no better than the wildest parts of Africa and which does not merit being better known'.

OVERLEAF, ABOVE Edward Lear, *The Temple of Apollo at Bassae*, 1854-5; oil on canvas, Fitzwilliam Museum, Cambridge. Painted in England from sketches done in Greece, this is one of the most powerful of the finished oils with which Lear hoped to make his name.

OVERLEAF, BELOW Edward Lear, *Parnassus*; watercolour, British Museum. Inscribed '12 April, 1849, noon', Lear characteristically includes in this work colour notes and other on-the-spot observations.

OVERLEAF, FAR RIGHT Edward Lear, *Choropiskeros*, Corfu, 1856; British Museum. The island of Corfu, a Turkish possession up until 1858, was a favourite destination for both Lear and other British travellers to the Balkans.

Parnassus
12 April 1849
noon

Fidénæ & Acqua & tora

Berat.
October. 1848.

132

Spain was as little visited as Greece up to the late eighteenth century, and initially deterred travellers with its reputation for bad roads, banditry, religious bigotry and general backwardness – aspects of Spain that would eventually constitute much of the country's romantic appeal. This appeal, ironically, grew rapidly from the 1780s onwards, when reforms initiated during the enlightened rule of Charles III were bringing Spain out of its previous isolation and into line with the most advanced countries in Europe. The Peninsular War of 1801-8 further helped to draw the attention of the rest of Europe to Spain, and provided, in its aftermath, an excuse for collectors to pick up works of art on the cheap: Britain and France managed between them to amass many of the greatest works by Zurbarán, Velázquez and Murillo.

The romantic image of Spain was consolidated between the 1820s and 1840s, when the country attracted some of the most influential of its early travellers, including Victor Hugo, Washington Irving, Prosper Mérimée, George Borrow, and Théophile Gautier. The key figure among the British Hispanists was Richard Ford, whose stay in Spain lasted only from 1831 to 1833, but led him to devote the rest of his life to Spanish matters, most notably the compilation of Murray's monumental *Handbook to Spain* (1st edition, 1845). An outstanding amateur draughtsman, Ford undertook lengthy sketching expeditions to parts of Spain that were visited by few other of his foreign contemporaries: he was, for instance, one of the first artists to sketch the Galician town of Santiago de Compostela, a place that had sunk into a long decline following the heyday of its medieval pilgrimage.

OPPOSITE Edward Lear, *Berat*, 1848; watercolour, the Houghton Library, Harvard University, Cambridge, Massachusetts. An Albanian scene featuring the kind of crowd which would periodically turn hostile on the artist.

John F. Lewis, *José María, Portrait of the Famous Robber . . . Drawn in my House at Seville*, 1833; pencil, Sir Brinsley Ford. Lewis' meeting with this Spanish Robin Hood was arranged by the great Hispanist, Richard Ford.

Joaquín Bécquer, *Portrait of Richard Ford in Majo Costume at the Feria of Mairena*, 1833; watercolour, Sir Brinsley Ford. Ford, a talented amateur artist as well as the author of the greatest guidebook ever written on Spain, had himself portrayed as a low-class dandy or *majo* by one of Seville's leading *costumbrista* painters.

Despite his broadly based interest in Spain, Ford was also responsible for promoting the still widely-held view that the most interesting and quintessentially Spanish part of the peninsular was Andalusia, where the Moorish influence was strongest. From the time of Ford, travellers crossing the Sierra Morena into Andalusia have had their heads turned at the pass of Despeñaperros and have succumbed on the other side to a Moorish intoxication that continues to this day to inspire effusive evocations of the region's jasmine-scented sensuality.

Two artist contemporaries of Ford who were to fall under the Moorish influence of Andalusia were John Lewis and David Roberts. Both painters had been encouraged to come to Spain by their teacher David Wilkie, whose visit to the Prado Museum in Madrid in 1828 had constituted a turning-point in his artistic development: Delacroix had seen Wilkie shortly after this visit and had wondered how 'a man with so true a genius, and almost arrived at old age, could be thus influenced by works so different from his own'. Spain was to have a similarly dramatic effect on Lewis and Roberts, inspiring in their case an interest in the Islamic world that would turn them into two of Britain's greatest Orientalists.

Lewis and Roberts, who were good friends, both came to Spain in 1832, but though they managed to keep in touch during their travels, they seem almost to have gone out of their way to avoid seeing each other, possibly because of an element of rivalry between them at this early stage in their careers. Lewis, the first to arrive in Spain, made watercolour copies of the old masters in the Prado before heading south to Andalusia, carrying with him a letter of introduction to Richard Ford. He finally met up with Ford in the latter's residence in Seville, which he reached shortly after the departure of Delacroix, then on a short trip to Spain from North Africa.

In a letter to the British ambassador in Madrid, Henry Addington, Ford described Lewis as a 'clever artist . . . [who] is about to make a sort of picturesque tour of Spain, having orders for young ladies' albums and from divers book-sellers who are illustrating Lord Byron'. Though Lewis made numerous sketches of landscapes and buildings, he was essentially a portraitist and figurative painter who would have found himself competing in Seville with the local school of *costumbristas* – artists who sold to passing tourists pictures of stereotypical Spanish types such as bull-fighters, *cigarreras*, bandits and the lower-class dandies known as *majos*. Thanks to Ford, Lewis was able to achieve something that none of these *costumbristas* had ever managed: he managed to meet and sketch the bandit king José María, an Andalusian Robin Hood whose image encapsulated foreigners' increasingly far-fetched notions of Spanish banditry. Lewis found a man who was five feet tall and bow-legged, but transformed him in his sketch into someone handsome and dashing.

Another of Lewis's works was a portrait of Ford's beautiful wife, Harriet, dressed in the costume of a *maja*, a costume which was frequently worn by British residents and travellers, supposedly as a way of avoiding the attention of bandits, but actually so as to indulge a love of dressing up. This love was later to be shown by Lewis in Egypt, and was indeed a characteristic of many of the Orientalists, who likewise fooled themselves into thinking that they donned exotic costumes so as to remain incognito in a foreign land.

Ford, with his extensive experience of sketching in Spain, would have warned

Lewis of the difficulties an artist was likely to face when working in the smaller towns and villages, and in particular of the very strong possibility of being mistaken for a spy. Lewis, like Roberts, kept to the main sites, the most important of which was the Alhambra in Granada, which by now had become the ultimate goal of travellers to Spain.

The Alhambra, for years as neglected and badly treated as the Parthenon was under Turkish occupancy, had begun to attract visitors once again in the late eighteenth century, the pioneering tourists being mainly British. The rediscovery of this monument coincided with the growing western interest in Islamic architecture, an interest that would change in the early nineteenth century from a primarily archaeological one to an increasingly sentimental one fired – in the case of Spain – by a Protestant desire to vaunt the virtues of a civilisation ousted by Catholicism.

John F. Lewis, *The Alhambra*, 1833; watercolour, British Museum. One of the most naturalistic of Lewis' generally fanciful portrayals of the Alhambra.

OPPOSITE Gentile Bellini, *Turkish Woman*; pen, British Museum. One of two surviving pen sketches dating from the artist's stay in Constantinople between 1479-81.

Interestingly, whereas the earliest prints of the Alhambra include the boldly classical palace built by Charles V in anachronistic proximity to the Nasrid residences, later views usually omit this entirely.

Lewis was among the many artists who idealised the Alhambra, and it has even been suggested that those who restored the building in the late nineteenth century referred on at least one occasion to his fanciful sketches rather than to the meticulous studies drawn up by his contemporary Owen Jones. But the artist who did most to capture and in turn to influence romantic imaginings of both the Alhambra and Spain itself was David Roberts.

Roberts' background as an artist was in architecture and scene-painting, and this would be reflected in his highly theatrical pictures, in which tiny figures are always set against structures of such exaggerated proportions that visitors to the actual places are liable to be disappointed. In his Spanish pictures further distortion is created by the fact that so many of these figures are monks or priests, thus reinforcing Protestant views about the fanaticism of the Spanish.

Roberts visited Granada in the summer, and found it 'so hot in the sun during the day that I cannot stand to sketch for ten minutes together, but am obliged to cross into the shade'. None the less no other place in Spain impressed him more, and he was able to write that it 'so far surpasses even the expectations I had formed of it great as these were'. The emotions that the Alhambra inspired in him resulted in illustrations of the building even more fanciful than those of Lewis. These works appeared in *The Tourist in Spain* (1835), the author of which, Thomas Roscoe, appears not to have visited the Alhambra itself but to have based his descriptions on Roberts' illustrations. Roberts transformed the Alhambra in accordance with Burke's theory of the Sublime, so that he not only imposed his customary exaggerations of scale onto the Hall of the Abencerrajes, but also gave this hall a gloomy, cavernous and gothic aspect. Roberts' portrayal of the building was no less of a romantic fantasy than the Alhambra tales of Washington Irving, and was comparably popular. It was from the money gained from these and other Spanish works that Roberts would be able to finance a long journey to the place which now loomed highest in his imagination – the Orient.

The Alhambra was perceived by most travellers in terms of some fairy tale, but the appeal of Spain generally, like that of Greece, came to seem less exotic to many of those who went on afterwards to North Africa and the Near East, where first-time visitors tended to react in the same way that Chassériau did on reaching Constantinople in 1845. 'I am', he exclaimed, 'in the Thousand and One Nights!'

The first destination of travellers to the Near East was usually Turkey, which was also the first oriental country to be popularised by western artists. The Venetian painter Gentile Bellini worked at the Court of Constantinople between 1479 and 1481, and is said to have painted erotic scenes for the harem of Sultan Mehmet II. Of greater consequence was the visit to Turkey in the late sixteenth century of the Danish artist Melchior Lorichs, who travelled as a member of a diplomatic mission sent by the Holy Roman Emperor to assess the Turkish threat to Europe. Lorichs's detailed record of Turkish life, *Turkish Customs and Costumes*, provided a major source

William Müller, *Travellers Khan, Smyrna*; watercolour, British Museum. From the eighteenth century onwards, Smyrna was a favourite base for foreign artists working in Asia Minor.

OPPOSITE Jean-Etienne Liotard, *Woman in Turkish Costume and her Servant*, 1742-3; pastel on parchment, Musée d'art et d'histoire, Geneva. Though once thought to have been executed towards the end of his four-year stay in Constantinople, this is now generally believed to be of slightly later date and to represent a European woman in costume; in any case it reinforces Liotard's reputation as one of the most outstanding of European pastelists.

book for sixteenth- and seventeenth-century artists, many of whom used scenes of Turkish inspiration to illustrate the travels of Marco Polo.

Exotic notions of Turkey and its people finally prompted in the early eighteenth century a widespread fashion for things Turkish, a fashion that gave rise to such diverse phenomena as Mozart's opera *Die Entführung aus dem Serail*, and Turkish figurines in Meissen porcelain. An artist who pioneered this taste for *turqueries* was the Valenciennes-born J.-B. Van Mour, who was brought to Turkey in around 1700 by the French ambassador M. de Ferriol, and who fell so much in love with the country that he remained there until his death in 1737. Enjoying the title of 'Painter-in-ordinary to the king of the Orient', Van Mour worked as a portraitist for Turks and visiting Europeans alike, but made his name originally with a commission from Ferriol to do a series of one hundred paintings (later engraved) of the most interesting customs of the Ottoman Empire. Whereas the original creators of chinoiserie had little visual evidence on which to base their vision of China, those associated with *turqueries* felt that they could rely heavily on the works of Van Mour, which seemed to gain in authenticity by the fact that the artist's standing at the sultan's court gave him access to aspects of Turkish life denied to other Europeans: he was one of the first Christians, for instance, to be able to witness the ceremonies of the whirling dervishes.

A more eccentric personality than Van Mour was the Genevese painter J.-E.

Liotard, who was also the first recorded artist in an exotic land wholly to immerse himself in local ways. Liotard had been working in Rome when he had made the acquaintance of the future Lord Bessborough, who proposed that he accompany him on a tour of the Near East. They set off in 1737, and visited among other places the town of Smyrna (now Izmir), which was the most popular Turkish destination after Constantinople, and a base from which members of the Society of Dilettanti and other archaeologically-minded Europeans could explore the ruins of Asia Minor. Liotard was particularly taken with Constantinople, and decided to stay on there after Lord Bessborough had returned to Europe. He grew his beard, wore Turkish clothes, and almost married a Turkish girl called Mimica.

Like Van Mour before him Liotard moved in the highest Turkish circles, and also received portrait commissions from European residents, one of whom was the erudite Gallard, the first translator of *The Thousand and One Nights*. When invited to diplomatic gatherings, Liotard changed at first into European costume, but eventually chose always to wear his more comfortable Turkish clothes, and continued to do so after he finally went back to Europe in 1743. With his turban, flowing robes and long Turkish beard, Liotard caused a sensation at the Court of Maria Theresa, and became known thereafter as 'le peintre Turc'.

Other French artists of the eighteenth century went to Turkey, and helped to turn the place into what a French art historian called a 'colony of the rococo'. Later it became a magnet to Orientalist painters, beginning with the pioneering artist of this movement, Alexandre-Gabriel Decamps, who, unimpressed with Greece in 1827, moved on to Asia Minor, and spent a long period working in an improvised studio at Smyrna, where he amassed motifs that would last him for the rest of his life.

Edward Lear also came to Turkey from Greece (in 1848), but reacted differently from other artists by not being immediately overwhelmed by his first impressions of the Orient; ' . . . the Bosphorus', he wrote, 'is the ghastliest humbug going! Compare the Straits of Menai or Southampton Waters or the Thames to it! It has neither form of hill nor character of any possible kind in its detail.' He was, admittedly, very ill at the time of his arrival in Turkey, and was to have a complete change of opinion the moment he began to recover. The exotic beauty of Constantinople, with its domes, minarets and cypresses, soon succeeded in winning him over completely, even if the Britishness of his humour always made him play down aspects of Turkey that would have inspired the most gushing reactions in other travellers. As the guest of the British ambassador and his wife, Lear was invited to witness the ceremony of 'foot-kissing' in the second court of the seraglio; no other Christians had been allowed into this ceremony before, but the account which he later gave of it was humorously down-to-earth, and brought out the monotony and drabness underlying the occasion's splendour and grandeur.

Even if Lear's abilities as a figurative painter had been sufficient to record what he had seen within the seraglio, his sense of humour precluded any serious interest in the type of subject-matter that obsessed most other artists in the Orient. The latter delighted in aspects of the Orient of which they were unlikely to have any direct experience, and that lived up to preconceptions of oriental cruelty, splendour, mystery and sensuality. Van Mour prefigured two of the more popular of these subjects when he painted one scene of a violent rebellion (in this case against Ahmed II) and another of a sultana in her bath. The hidden world of the seraglio, the harem, and the Turkish bath held a particular fascination for artists, not least for the opportunity of painting voluptuous female bodies in various states of undress. Few if any of the artists would have seen a high-ranking Islamic woman without a veil, let alone been allowed to portray one in such a state (the female portraits by Lorichs are almost certainly imaginary). And not even the most privileged male artists such as Van Mour would have been allowed to roam freely around the harem and the baths.

The only westerner known to have visited a women's Turkish bath in the eighteenth century was Lady Mary Wortley Montagu, who went to those of Sofia in 1717, and gave an account of naked beauties that would provide the inspiration for numerous later depictions of the subject, including the famous *Bain Turc* by Ingres. The prolific nineteenth-century Orientalist Jean-Léon Gérôme gained entry into the celebrated baths at Bursa, but did so at a time when no one was around; the sketches he executed there were later used for finished paintings necessitating Parisian models and considerable artistic licence. The reality of the Turkish baths was almost certainly less glamorous than was conveyed either by painters or even by Lady Mary Wortley Montagu, who, for all her complaints about fanciful portrayals of the Orient, seems to have idealised what she saw in Sofia. A more truthful account was probably that of the wife of the French geographer Hommaire de Hell, whose perfumed visions of harem life vanished entirely when confronted in the Bursa baths by four or five crouching women emanating 'the most depressing vulgarity'.

The secret, inaccessible nature of so much of the Orient helped to maintain the romantic illusions of westerners, as did the wealth of exotic costumes, pungent smells, and strange sights and sounds that relentlessly confronted the traveller. Those who first experienced the Orient in Turkey were able at least to prepare themselves for the strangeness of their new environment in the course of the long journey to get there. However, to those reaching the Orient merely by crossing the narrow straits of Gibraltar the cultural shock between west and east was – and still is – an enormous one. Spain might have been 'half African', as Hugo noted in *Les Orientales*, but Africa was 'half Asian'. Even those whose heads had been turned at Despeñaperros, such as the French painter Alfred Dehodencq, did not expect to react so strongly on coming to Morocco from Spain. 'I thought I was going crazy', said Dehodencq in 1853.

Most of the travellers who visited the south of Spain in the nineteenth century made short trips into Morocco, and most of them were as astonished as Dehodencq by the country. Richard Ford came here in the spring of 1833, and thought the place was a paradise, particularly in comparison with Gibraltar, from where he had sailed. 'I need not tell you', he wrote to Addington,

how great is the change on landing [in Tangier], greater than that between Dover and Calais. I will not say that, on coming from Spain, it is coming from civilization to barbarism, it being well known that Africa begins at the Pyrenees; but still the change is of turbans for hats . . . camels for mules . . . wild Arabs in their peaked Jellibeas [*sic*] for monks, and is sufficiently striking.

David Roberts, *The Citadel of Tangier*, 1833; watercolour, British Museum. One of the few surviving works dating from the artist's first visit to North Africa.

John Lewis and David Roberts went to Morocco from Gibraltar at about the same time as Ford, and had their first real if brief encounter with the Orient there. 'I find myself in a new world', wrote Roberts ecstatically from Tangier in March 1833, 'I thought Spain different, but this excels all I have seen. Yesterday was the market-day – an African market; and I am so bewildered that I cannot trust myself to write about it . . .' Tangier offered a vast amount of material to such artists as Roberts, and also had a history of tolerance towards westerners. Outside the city, however, protective measures were needed, and sketching was difficult: there were no foreign garrisons to reassure the visitor as there were in neighbouring Algeria. Roberts, in visiting what he described as the 'more strictly Moorish towns of the interior', fortunately relished rather than cursed the difficulties he had to face, and delighted in telling a friend that had he seen him disguised in Arabian costume and in the company of his mounted Moorish guide and bodyguard, 'you could have said I was somebody'. He also boasted, as he would later do in Egypt, that he was the first artist

to sketch in this part of Africa: what he should have said was that he was one of the earliest to do so independent of a diplomatic or scientific mission.

Delacroix had preceded Roberts to Morocco by exactly a year, but had come here as a late replacement for the painter Isabey in the suite of the Comte de Mornay. Mornay's mission was to have an agreement signed between the French and the Moroccan sultan, Abd al-Rhaman, whose cooperation was important in securing French interests in Algeria. Their first stop was Tangier, where Delacroix was suitably enthralled by the costumes and colours, and felt compelled to adopt the medium of watercolour to do these justice. As with many other travellers to the Orient, Delacroix found that the appearance of the locals fulfilled his imaginings of what the ancient Greeks and Romans must have looked like: the 'Greeks' who were featured in the works of the Neo-classical painter David seemed to him laughable in comparison. Sketching these people posed of course its problems, though he usually got over these in Tangier by the offering of *baqshish*; moreover, as with other

Eugène Delacroix, *Sketch for the Women of Algiers*, British Museum. This sketch for the famous canvas in the Louvre was reputedly inspired by a visit to a harem in Algiers.

Alexandre Decamps, *Animal Studies, North Africa;* pencil, British Museum. Decamps was content merely to sketch some of the animals he encountered in North Africa; other artists felt the need to bring them back home to serve as models.

OPPOSITE Eugène Delacroix, *Seated Moroccan,* 1832; British Museum. The sketches executed by Delacroix on his Moroccan journey have a vivid presence that is rarely equalled in the work of the other Orientalists.

Orientalists throughout North Africa and the Near East, he was able to find willing and beautiful female models among the town's large Jewish population.

The real difficulties came when the Comte de Mornay's suite finally reached Meknes, where the sultan had his residence. Delacroix had set off to Meknes in a state of considerable anticipation, but was soon reduced on arrival to feelings of abject boredom. To sketch openly here was a virtual impossibility, while anyone who went around dressed as a Christian was liable to be subjected to insults or worse: he became a virtual prisoner in his quarters, and could not even step out onto his terrace without running the risk of being stoned or shot at. All this was particularly frustrating, as 'at every step one sees ready-made pictures, which would bring fame and fortune to twenty generations of painters'.

Matter improved when the Comte de Mornay's suite moved on from Meknes and eventually reached Algiers, which since 1830 had been much frequented by French artists, many of whom were being sent there for propaganda purposes by Louis-Philippe: the town was only a day's journey by ship from Marseilles, and thus the easiest point of entry into the Orient after Tangier. It was here that Delacroix reputedly enjoyed the ultimate of oriental experiences by being admitted into a harem; but the story of his harem visit, and of his recourse afterwards to sorbets to calm himself down, is almost certainly apochryphal.

Algeria had much of exotic appeal, but the 'Haussmannisation' to which it was

OPPOSITE Jacques-Louis Denon, *Festival in the Harem*, c.1798; pen, British Museum. Although this Cairo scene was probably drawn from imagination, Egyptian dancing girls had previously been sketched from life by the Danish artist, Georg Baurenfeind.

OPPOSITE BELOW Jacques-Louis Denon, *Numibian Women*, c.1798; pen, British Museum. One of many sketches done on Denon's journey into Upper Egypt.

being subjected by the French after 1830 was such that artists and visitors were forced to venture even further into the interior in their search for uncorrupted scenes. One of the more adventurous of these artists was Fromentin, who was seized from the moment of his arrival in Algeria in 1846 by 'that indefinable and unmistakable smell of the Orient'. Escaping from the colonial towns of the coast he travelled inland in search 'of a more or less intact Arabian town', and discovered on camel-back the haunting beauty of the Sahara. The monotony and emptiness of the desert expanses made him susceptible to every subtle variation in light and colour, while the experience of being bathed all day in brilliant sunshine induced in him 'a sort of inebriation'. His passion for this landscape, and his dedication to recording it in words and pictures was shared by few others of his generation; but the taste for a pseudo-Bedouin lifestyle he acquired in the process was common to many Orientalists, in particular those who were active in Egypt and the Holy Land.

Of all the oriental countries that attracted artists, by far the most popular was Egypt, which is significantly at the junction of North Africa and the Near East. The rediscovery of ancient Egypt provided the initial impulse for artists to come here, one of the first to do so being Richard Dalton, who in 1749 accompanied Lord Charlemont on a tour of this country. The crudeness of the watercolours that resulted from this trip (now in the Royal Collection) might explain why other British touring aristocrats in eighteenth-century Egypt favoured Italian rather than British draughtsmen. The Bolognese artist Luigi Balugari worked in the 1760s and 1770s for the intrepid adventurer Robert Bruce, while in 1792 the Rome-trained Luigi Mayer was employed by the British ambassador in Constantinople, Sir Robert Ainslie, to undertake the first detailed pictorial record of the antiquities, landscapes and people of Egypt.

The efforts of the likes of Dalton, Balugari and Mayer were diminished in 1798 by the arrival in Egypt of Napoleon and his large team of artists headed by Jacques-Louis Denon. Until this time Europeans had taken an interest in the monuments of ancient Egypt mainly because they believed, mistakenly, that these had been an enormous influence on the development of classical art and architecture; Denon, however, seems to have appreciated the Egyptian monuments independent of any classical context, and was accordingly more rigorous in his recording of them. With the consequent development of Egyptology numerous other artists and archaeologists descended on Egypt, one of these being Henry Salt, a draughtsman and portraitist who was appointed British Consul in Egypt in 1815 and was thereafter contracted to collect Egyptian antiquities for the British Museum. An especially large team of artists was assembled in the 1820s and 1830s by the collector and scholar Thomas Hay, among whom were the Alhambra draughtsman Owen Jones and the future recorder of Mayan antiquities Frederick Catherwood.

The growing appeal of Egypt coincided, as did that of Spain, with the dramatic modernisation of the country. The main reforms were initiated during the long, enlightened if also ruthless rule of Muhammad Ali, an adventurer of Albanian origin who came to power in Egypt in 1805 and who, six years later, disposed of his remaining Mamluk enemies by the time-honoured ruse of inviting them all to a banquet. Muhammad Ali enlisted French and other European experts to remodel

his army and to establish new industries in the country; at the same time he alarmed the west by such acts of defiance towards his nominal rulers, the Ottomans, as seizing Syria in 1830. The continuing stability of the Ottoman Empire was of especial importance to the British: on it depended the future success of the overland route to India.

This route was finally established in 1840, the year when joint British, French and Austrian action forced the Egyptians out of Syria, and when the newly constituted Peninsular and Oriental Steam Navigation Company received a five year contract from the British government to carry the mails to India. Excellent communications were developed between Alexandria and Suez so as to link up with a regular steamship service from London to Alexandria, and from Suez to Bombay; the luxurious Hôtel d'Orient was built in Cairo, as were many other new hotels that helped to turn Egypt into one of the most comfortable of the world's exotic destinations. The brilliant entrepreneur behind the whole enterprise was Lieutenant Thomas Waghorn, a man whose energy inspired Thackeray to comment in 1844 that 'Wag has conquered the pyramids themselves, dragged the unwieldy structures a month nearer England than they were, and brought the country along with them.'

Thousands of British and other travellers now visited Egypt, and, inevitably, there were those who criticised the effects on the country of the modernisation that had encouraged them to come here. The Orient was in danger of losing its exoticism, a danger which would increase with the opening of the Suez Canal in 1862, the year of Egypt's independence. 'The barriers between East and West have been broken down', commented one French contemporary with an enthusiasm which might have alarmed the more romantically-inclined.

The first important artists to work in Egypt were those who came here from the 1830s onwards, from the beginnings of the country's first major period of westernisation. The French painter Prosper Marilhat, whose oriental canvases would have such an impact on Gautier and others, arrived in Egypt in 1831 in the course of a scientific expedition led by the botanist Baron Karl von Hugel. The Baron and his party continued their journey as far as India, but Marilhat stayed on absorbed in Cairo, where he fell deeper into an oriental intoxication which might have contributed to the madness from which he would die at the age of thirty-six.

While in Cairo, Marilhat executed a portrait of Muhammad Ali, who would also be the subject of works by David Wilkie and his two pupils David Roberts and John Lewis. Wilkie received the commission to paint the Pasha in 1841, at the end of a tour in the Near East which had begun the year before in Turkey, where, ironically, he had celebrated on canvas the news of the Pasha's defeat in Syria. Wilkie had reached Egypt at the same time as Lewis, but two years after the departure of Roberts, who is usually claimed as one of the first independent British artists to go there.

Roberts' friend and biographer James Ballantine described Roberts' visit to the Near East in 1838-9 as 'the great central episode of his artistic life', and the fulfilment of a childhood dream. The nucleus of this journey had been its Egyptian part, which had begun in Alexandria in the September of 1838 and had continued along the Nile to Cairo and beyond. Roberts wondered what the British public would make of his drawings of the pyramids ('I am the first English artist who has been here'), and believed that the ground in Cairo 'was equally untrodden'. Cairo, which was described by Hommaire de Hell as 'a labyrinth for the eye and the mind', made an enormous impression on Roberts, who found 'such glorious subjects' in the city's picturesque maze of streets that he foresaw 'ample employment for years to come'. He also confessed that 'these narrow, crowded streets render it very difficult to make drawings, for in addition to the curiosity of the Arabs, you run a risk of being squeezed to a mummy by the loaded camels, who, although they are picturesque in appearance, are ugly customers to jostle'.

There were also the problems of visiting and sketching the city's various mosques – problems that Roberts attempted to overcome by assuming Turkish costume, shaving off his whiskers, and foresaking brushes made of hog's hair. But despite these efforts to ingratiate himself in local ways, and despite his fascination with the oriental world, he was repelled by the squalor and decay he saw around him, and blamed this on Islam, 'a religion of barbarism'. The way his judgement of Egypt continued to be affected by British prejudices was also reflected in his attitude towards Egypt's ancient monuments . . . 'they strike the beholder with wonder, but not with pleasure', he noted, 'an ivy mantelled tower with a brawling bairn conveys I think a more pleasurable sensation than the land of the Pharaohs and all its wonders'.

John Lewis, who came to Egypt after extensive travels in the Balkans and Turkey, had more opportunity to get to know this country than had Roberts or indeed any other British artist: he stayed in Cairo for ten years, and immersed himself in local life as fully as Liotard had done in Constantinople. 'He was living', wrote the Governor of Madras to Lewis's brother Frederick in 1845, 'in the most Ottoman quarter of Cairo – in a house which might supply material for half the Oriental Annuals and manuals of eastern architecture that appear in London and Paris'. This vast mansion, with its shuttered galleries, array of servants, and camels in its courtyard, enabled Lewis to find hundreds of exotic motifs without having to go into the streets and risk the problems that Roberts had faced: in one of his works he even pretended that it was the house of the Coptic Patriarch of Cairo.

The proverbial oriental indolence that Lewis portrayed in his exquisitely detailed interiors seems also to have affected the artist himself, to judge from the accounts of two of those who visited him at his home. Sir Thomas Phillips, travelling around the Near East in 1844 with the psychopathic artist Richard Dadd, reported that Lewis 'has not been very usefully employed hitherto'. 'A brilliant but idle lotus-eater' was how Lewis was perceived in this same year by Thackeray, whose long and vivid description of his visit to the artist's home makes this sound like an audience with some oriental potentate. After being led by a series of servants through the many rooms of the house, Thackeray finally reached a large, mysteriously lit hall, where he was made to wait on a divan until the eventual arrival of a man robed in yellow, with a shaved head swathed in a red 'tarboosh', and a way of summoning domestics with a clap of the hands. Lewis, Thackeray revealed, had always been a dandy in the London clubs, but mere dandyism had now given way to something else. He had wholly embraced a world of oriental make-believe.

John F. Lewis, *Study for Courtyard of the Coptic Patriarch's House*; oil on canvas, Tate Gallery. The scene represented is in fact the courtyard of Lewis' Cairo home, which was described in great detail by Thackeray.

'There have never been, & there never will be, any works depicting Oriental life . . . *so* beautiful and excellent', opined Edward Lear of the works of Lewis, an artist whose temperament, way of life, and perception of the Orient could hardly have been more different from his own. Lear first came to Egypt in 1849, and found that it lacked the 'romance or the variety and interest of Greece, but what *there is* is so

perfect in its own particular beauty'. With his enormous straw hat, and bulbous bright red nose, Lear cut a rather less dashing figure than Lewis, and was ill at ease in this environment of lonely, unchanging landscapes, and unfamiliar, hugely proportioned monuments. 'I am really so surprised', he wrote after a visit to the pyramids, 'I don't know what to do.'

Thomas Seddon, *Jerusalem*; oil on canvas, Tate Gallery. Seddon, who travelled in the Holy Land with his fellow Pre-Raphaelite, Holman Hunt, here portrays Jerusalem from the viewpoint most favoured by artists.

On a return visit to Egypt in 1853, Lear met up in Cairo with Holman Hunt and Thomas Seddon, to whom he was able to proffer his 'advice as an experienced traveller'. Hunt and Seddon, with their Pre-Raphaelite obsession with realism, belonged to a generation of British artists whose main motive in travelling to Egypt and the Holy Land was to search out authentic settings for Biblical scenes. They had little interest in modern Egypt, which was viewed by Seddon in terms of an encroaching westernisation responsible for the construction of 'the vilest possible copies of European [buildings]'. At the same time they were prevented by their Christian and European prejudices from wholeheartedly enjoying the country's ancient past. 'Merely colossal tombs of pride' was how Hunt regarded the pyramids, which he further described as 'extremely ugly blocks . . . arranged with most unpicturesque taste'.

Another artist of this generation was Frederick Goodall, who, armed with letters of introduction from his old friend David Roberts, came to Egypt in 1858 with the sole intention 'to paint scriptural subjects'. His travelling companion, Sir Lewis Pelly, was to tell him many years afterwards that 'he never saw any one so nearly cracked as I seemed to be immediately after the landing at Alexandria'. The delirious excitement Goodall experienced on arrival in Egypt was maintained throughout his stay in Cairo, and withstood the inconveniences of having to sketch in the crowded streets under the protection of an armed guard who occasionally fell asleep, thus leaving the artist to the mercy of stones and shouts of 'Pig!', 'Pig of a Christian!'

To be able to work in greater comfort, Goodall adopted Lewis's solution of renting a picturesque old house where he could paint camels, people and other motifs in the safety of its courtyard. However, he did not assume local customs in the same way that Lewis had done, and remained proudly and resolutely British in his behaviour. For Christmas in Cairo he even attempted to make Christmas pudding, and was not deterred by the discovery that the suet available here was taken steaming from the animal and was thus difficult to chop: the resulting pudding was so much of a success that the painter Carl Haag, with whom he shared his Cairo house, congratulated him for 'having reminded him so appropriately of Old England'.

Though Thackeray considered that an 'artist's fortune could be made in Cairo', the rapid growth of the modern city and the invasion of artists and tourists led a number of painters to become dissatisfied with the place, and to go deeper into Egypt in search of adventure and an unspoilt Orient. One such painter was Marc-Gabriel Gleyre, who, as early as 1836, left Cairo after complaining that it was 'impossible to find a place where you can escape from the company of artists – they have spoilt Cairo for me'. Gleyre sailed down the Nile into Upper Egypt, where the great temples at Karnak, Luxor and Abu Simbel awaited him. He thought at times that he had rediscovered the Garden of Eden, but was left depressed by the 'arid, black mountains of Nubia', which made him pine for 'beautiful Italy'. Eventually he fell victim to poverty, exhaustion and ill health, and would have lost his sight from ophthalmia had not his pet monkey licked his eyes up to the time he could visit a doctor; he returned to Europe 'in a state a thousand times worse than that of the prodigal son'.

Thomas Seddon, illustration from J. P. Seddon's *Memoir and Letters of the late Thomas Seddon*, London, 1858. Seddon, whilst engaged in painting the pyramids, is approached by a local woman who begs him to write a letter petitioning her husband to stop beating her.

Upper Egypt was the main destination for artists travelling outside Cairo, and many of them embarked on their Nile trip as if undertaking a major journey of exploration. David Roberts emulated the example of other British travellers by placing the Union Jack on top of the boat he had commandeered; he also revealed a certain macho boastfulness in confessing to Ballantine that 'with the exception of swarms of mosquitoes, fleas, bugs, lizards etc., from whom I suffered martyrdom, running over me all night, eating my victuals, and even nibbling my straw hat, on the whole I was tolerably comfortable . . .' Yet Roberts and the great majority of his artist contemporaries went no further than the Nile's second cataract, and thus kept to a stretch of the river which was already becoming so popular with tourists that Thomas Cook's would soon be organising luxury cruises for passengers requiring daily newspapers, morning porridge, and afternoon tea.

For the romantic traveller escaping from the modern world the most promising direction in which to head from Cairo was east into the Sinai desert. Marilhat, Roberts, Lewis, Gérôme, Seddon, Hunt, Dadd, Lear, Goodall and William Bartlett were among the many who got to know – as Fromentin did in Algeria – the thrills of desert travel in the company of camels and Bedouin guides. Lewis confided to Thackeray that even Cairo was too civilised for him and that

the great pleasure of pleasures was life outside Cairo in the desert – under the tents with still more nothing to do than in Cairo; now smoking, now cantering on Arabs, and no crowd to jostle you; solemn contemplations of the stars at night, as the camels were picketed, and the fires and the pipes were lighted.

A more sober appraisal of this lifestyle was given in 1840 by Bartlett, who found that he lost all energy to sketch after a day spent on a camel, and that his romantic notions of the Orient were partially dispelled by the 'vermin-infested bedouin', with whom he recommended travellers 'not to *associate too* closely'. Bartlett also exposed the pretentions of those westerners who crossed the desert disguised as Arabs. 'As for dress', he said, 'it is decidedly better, both for comfort and safety, to travel in a light European costume, the English name being sufficient protection'.

David Roberts, *Coffee Shop, Jaffa*, 1838; watercolour, British Museum. On his way to Jerusalem Roberts passed through the Palestinian town of Jaffa, where he executed this unusually intimate work.

Many of the artists who experienced what Roberts called the 'sublimity and desolation' of the Sinai desert continued north to the Holy Land and the Levant – destinations that were also visited by those intrepid enough to undertake the gruelling overland journey to Cairo from Constantinople. The Holy Land came into fashion after Chateaubriand's visit there in 1825, though many would be disappointed by Jerusalem itself, which had for Lear a melancholy beauty from afar while being 'physically . . . the foulest and odiousest place on earth'.

There was the added frustration of the near total inaccessibility of one of the most famous of the city's Biblical sites, the Dome of the Rock, a place associated as much with Mohammed as with Christ. While working for Robert Hay in 1833, the topographical artist Frederick Catherwood was commissioned by Muhammad Ali to inspect this and other mosques with a view to assess what repairs were necessary. To avoid the fate of those foreigners who had reportedly been put to death for merely entering the site's outer courtyard, Catherwood went dressed as an Egyptian officer. An ugly scene none the less ensued when he sat down to sketch, and he might well have lost his life had not the Governor of Jerusalem intervened and convinced the crowd of the value of what Catherwood was doing. Christian access to Muslim sites throughout the Orient would greatly improve with the increased western presence here; but it was not until 1859 that the first watercolour was painted within the Dome – the artist responsible, Carl Haag, had to obtain the necessary permission to do so through the intercession of Queen Victoria. When, three years later, the

Reverend Albert Isaacs was allowed to take the first photographs of the Dome, the priests and guardians of the site had apparently to be 'locked up' before his visit in case 'they might revenge with their daggers the attempt to desecrate the holy ground with the footsteps of the infidel'.

For those travelling overland between Cairo and Constantinople, there were three isolated archaeological sites that serious artists made every attempt to visit. One of these was Palmyra in Syria, which Carl Haag was so keen on seeing that he said he would go there even 'if I am a ruined man all my life, or if I walk there in Bedouin sandals'. Another Syrian site was Baalbek, which David Roberts visited under rainy conditions in the spring of 1839. By now Baalbek was attracting a fair number of tourists, but this did not stop Roberts from identifying himself with the place's pioneering explorers, whose names he included in his famous canvas of the *Gateway of the Temple of Bacchus*.

Improved policing in the last days of the Ottoman Empire lessened the danger of being attacked by Arab tribesmen on the way to places such as Palmyra and Baalbek. However, a very real possibility of such attacks remained for those who visited the remote Jordanian site of Petra, a place that overwhelmed the traveller with its haunting strangeness and rugged sandstone setting. William Bartlett spent one of the most exciting days of his life here; others almost lost their lives. Gérôme, travelling around Jordan in a caravan of forty-seven camels, twenty servants, and six companions, had a narrow escape near Petra from one of the local tribes that

Richard Dadd, *The Halt in the Desert*; watercolour, British Museum. In this recently discovered work, based on a Middle Eastern trip made by the artist with Sir Thomas Phillips in 1844, Dadd brilliantly captures the mystery and adventure that desert travel offered westerners.

Edward Lear, *Richard Burton in Oriental Costume*, 1853; watercolour, the Houghton Library, Harvard University, Cambridge, Massachusetts. Sketched when Lear was in Cairo with Seddon and Holman Hunt, this shows the great Arabian explorer dressed in the disguise he used to reach Mecca.

Cairo Dec. 23. 1853

Jules Laurens, *Winter in Persia*; Hôtel de Ville, Bagnères de Bigorre. A memory of Laurens' nightmarish journey to Tehran in 1847 in the company of the distinguished geographer, Hommaire de Hell.

demanded dues from passing strangers. A similar fate befell Edward Lear, who became so convinced that his end was at hand that he scrawled his name on one of Petra's ruins so that a search party would know of his latest whereabouts; in the end he was merely stripped of almost everything he possessed by the mob of two hundred Arabs who set upon him.

Any journey in exotic lands carried with it a certain element of risk, and there were several artists who came to the Orient who never returned to Europe – David Wilkie, Thomas Seddon and William Bartlett all contracted fatal illnesses at the very end of tours to the Near East. The travellers who faced the greatest dangers were those who journeyed into Arabia, where, for once, dressing up in Arab garb was usually essential, as was the case with Richard Burton making his way in secret to Mecca in 1853. These travellers tended almost exclusively to be professional adventurers rather than artists, though both Burton and the similarly intrepid Lady Anne Blunt were the authors of numerous amateur and furtively executed sketches. One of the only topographical draughtsmen known to have worked in Arabia was also perhaps the earliest, Georg Wilhelm Baurenfeind, who accompanied the ill-fated scientific expedition to the Near East led in 1761-7 by the Danish scientists Niebuhr and Forskall. While crossing Arabia the members of this expedition succumbed one by one to illness until eventually only Niebuhr was left.

In Persia, where a less rigid form of Shia Islam was practised, sketching con-

Robert Kerr Porter, *Third Bas-relief at Nackshi-Roystami*, 1817-20; pen and wash, the British Library. Sir Robert, in military uniform, is shown sketching one of the most famous of Persian sites.

ditions for artists were in some ways easier than elsewhere in the Near East. The physical hardships, however, were even worse, as was illustrated in the journey of the main French Orientalist to have come to Persia, Jules Laurens, who travelled around the country in 1847 in the company of the geographer Hommaire de Hell. The two men, on a mission from the French government, chose to go to Teheran by way of Trebizond, Erzeroum and Tabriz, a route that had rarely been attempted before by Europeans. Though they were travelling in July, their journey entailed climbing into the snows, which left Hommaire de Hell temporarily snow-blind and reduced Laurens to such a state of fever and weakness that he had to use his easel as a crutch as he bravely continued to sketch at every stop. Teheran provided at first a wonderful respite after this nightmare of a journey, but threatening demands from people wanting Laurens to paint their portraits eventually forced them to leave the city and head south through the desert in the middle of August. Suffering from heat and dysentery, Hommaire de Hell died soon afterwards, looked after by a distraught Laurens, who persevered for a while on his own in Persia before choosing to return home after one of this country's many sudden changes of regime.

The army rather than the art school furnished most of the draughtsmen who recorded Persia: Colonel Colombari, famous for his system of loading cannons on the back of camels, did many sketches here, as did Sir Robert Kerr Porter, whose Persian drawings comprise the finest and most detailed British record of the country in the nineteenth century. Travelling with the army, or in a military uniform (as in Sir Robert's case), was sometimes the only solution for those intending to paint or sketch in the more dangerous outposts of the Orient. Thus it was only through joining in 1851 the armies of the Tsar that the Russian artist and Gérôme pupil Vereshchagin could visit an area remoter still than Persia and as yet unvisited by the Orientalist: the deserts of Bokkhara.

A taste for exotic travel inevitably encourages a desire to visit ever more distant lands. For those whose appetites had been whetted by their experiences in North Africa and the Near East, the obvious course of action was to continue heading eastwards, at least as far as India, where such artists as Lear would find themselves in a world stranger and more colourful than any they had known before.

2

India

George Chinnery, *Self-portrait*; British Museum. Chinnery drew this when still in India, before he developed the notorious paunch of his later years.

OPPOSITE George Chinnery *Sketches of Bathers, April 18, 1813;* the British Library Oriental and India Office Collections. An example of Chinnery's telescopic view of Indian life, these sketches were possibly done at Benares.

David Roberts, contemplating the desert near Cairo, wondered if it would 'ever again become the haunt of men'. The thoughts entertained by him and fellow British travellers to the Near East were not always oriental fantasies but embraced as well the possibility that Egypt would one day be incorporated within the British Empire and become a focus of commercial activity comparable to India.

Long before Orientalism was established as a pictorial and literary fashion, British artists had been going to India, spurred on not by chimerical visions but by the prospect of actively participating in the profitable imperial process. The artists mirrored the remarkable flowering of British interest in India, and had already produced by the mid-nineteenth century a pictorial record of the country far more extensive than that of any other exotic land under western domination.

Britain had been trading with India since the founding of the East India Company in 1600, and had acquired its first Indian possession in 1662 through receiving Bombay as part of the dowry of Catherine of Braganza. Bombay proved a more lasting legacy of this dowry than Tangier had been, and formed the kernel of an empire that rapidly grew in the course of the eighteenth century, when British trading interests in India were finally expanded into political ones.

In the last quarter of the eighteenth century, under the leadership of the learned first Governor-General of Bengal, Warren Hastings, British rule in India reached an enlightened peak. The British residents of this period attempted to a certain extent to adjust to the Indian environment. Some took to the wearing of Indian costumes, decorated their homes with numerous Indian works of art, and even married or lived openly with Indian woman. A scholarly interest in the religions, history and culture of India was also developed under the impetus of such remarkable figures as the Supreme Court Judge of Calcutta, Sir William Jones, whose activities as first president of the Royal Asiatic Society (founded in Calcutta in 1784) earned him the title of 'father of oriental Studies'.

The much publicised defeat in 1792 of the powerful Tipu Sultan of Mysore greatly extended British dominion in the south of India, while the capture of Delhi in 1803 helped open up new regions in the north. The empire continued to be enlarged in the early nineteenth century, but at the same time the British and the Indians drifted further and further apart. A greater moral and social censoriousness on the part of the rapidly expanding British community led this community to live in an ever more isolated world. Mixed marriages came to be frowned upon, and the donning of formal western attire – so impractical in the hot conditions – seemed now far preferable than 'going native'. Enlightened figures such as Warren Hastings were

137

April 18'
1813

At Sultah Ghaut June 30. 1813.

George Chinnery, *At Sultah Ghaut, June 30, 1813*; pencil, the British Library Oriental and India Office Collections. Detailed drawings such as these reveal Chinnery as one of the great landscape draughtsmen of the early nineteenth century.

succeeded by the likes of Thomas Babington Macaulay, who ruthlessly imposed English as the institutional language of India while denying any validity in the study of Sanskrit and Arabic; later he went on to attack Hinduism as 'hideous and grotesque and ignoble'. The Indian Mutiny of 1857 was the inevitable outcome of the widening rift between the British and their subjects.

The vast body of paintings, drawings and prints recording India was essentially compiled in little more than a century: there is far less material of this kind after 1857 and virtually none before the mid-eighteenth century other than the crude engravings illustrating some of the early travel books. The most interesting period in the artistic representation of India coincided with those years of intense intellectual and scientific enquiry into the Asiatic world initiated during the governorship of Warren Hastings. In the preface to his *A Picturesque Voyage to India by Way of China* (1810), the artist Thomas Daniell stressed how in the late eighteenth century the

passion for discovery, originally kindled by the thirst for gold, was exalted to a higher and nobler aim than commercial speculations . . . The shores of Asia have been invaded by a race of students with no rapacity but for lettered relics: by naturalists, whose cruelty extends not to one human inhabitant; by philosophers extirpations of error, and the diffusion of truth. It remains for the artist to claim his part in these guiltless spoliations, and to transport to Europe the picturesque beauties of those favoured regions.

Money none the less played a significant role in luring artists to India in the first

place. The fabled riches of some of the Indian Maharajahs promised more generous sources of patronage than were generally available in late eighteenth-century Britain. Furthermore there was also the newly acquired wealth of some of the East India Company employees, which attracted from the 1750s onwards not only a growing number of artists from Britain but also numerous unmarried women. One person who succeeded in finding both artistic employment and a wealthy husband was the miniaturist Martha Isaacs, who painted portraits of British residents in Calcutta before eventually marrying a 'Mr. Higgison' – 'a gentleman high in the Company's Civil Service and of high fortune.'

The earliest professional British artists to work in eighteenth-century India were portraitists rather than landscapists. The first to come here was Tilly Kettle, who lived in India from 1769 to 1776, staying initially at Madras, where he painted portraits both of East India Company servants and of the Nawab of the Carnatic and his family. Afterwards he moved to Lucknow, where he worked for the Nawab of Oudh, and took an Indian wife ('*bibi*'), with whom he had two daughters. The money he made in India was a spur to other British artists, including Johann Zoffany, who, after a prodigious early success in Britain, had fallen on hard times. Zoffany came to India in 1783 and stayed for five years, mainly in Calcutta, where he enjoyed the patronage of Warren Hastings; he also made three visits to Lucknow, where he received commissions from the Nawab of Oudh as well as from European

William Hodges, *View of Benares*, 1781; oil on canvas, the British Library Oriental and India Office Collections. One of the oil paintings made for Warren Hastings from sketches done on the spot.

residents such as the flamboyant French adventurer Claude Martin – the subject of one of his livelier Indian 'conversation pieces'.

Both Kettle and Zoffany painted an Indian subject which was to become almost as popular with artists in India as harem scenes were to painters in North Africa and the Near East – the '*sati*' or ritual burning of a widow on her deceased husband's funeral pyre. Whether or not Kettle and Zoffany actually witnessed such a ceremony (and this is highly unlikely), they made the scene appeal to eighteenth-century western sensibilities by transforming it into some secular Sacrifice of Iphigenia. The pictorial, idealising conventions of eighteenth-century Europe also affected, not unnaturally, their Indian portraits, which lack the striking immediacy of many of the works by the hybrid Indian artists known as the 'Company School': thus while Kettle executed portraits in a Van Dyke mode, he was shown by one of the Company artists looking like a 1960s' rock star, complete with long hair, glasses, and side burns.

If the outlook for the portraitist in late eighteenth-century Britain was so bad as to force an artist of the calibre of Zoffany to work in India, the situation was even worse for landscapists. Landscape art in Britain, then in its infancy, was dominated by Richard Wilson, one of whose followers, William Hodges, experienced his first lucky break after being invited in 1772 as official artist on Captain Cook's second voyage to the Pacific (see pages 84-9). A taste for exotic travel clearly stayed with Hodges, for in 1780 he became the first professional British artist to visit India. 'The clear blue cloudless sky', he noted on arrival,

the polished white buildings, the bright sandy beach, the dark green sea, present a combination totally new to the eye of an Englishman, just arrived from London, who, accustomed to the sight of rolling masses of clouds floating in a damp atmosphere, cannot but contemplate the difference with delight, and the eye thus gratified, the mind assumes a gay and tranquil habit, analagous to the pleasing objects with which it is surrounded.

Hodges was initially based in Madras, but discovered that he was unable to go further than the city's immediate outskirts on account of the Second Madras War: 'The opportunities that offer to a painter are few', he commented, 'in a country which is over-run by an active enemy.' After being confined to Madras for a year, he went on to Calcutta, where he found a friend, patron, and fellow Indian enthusiast in Warren Hastings. Hastings – Hodges' keenest supporter – commissioned all of the artist's major oils, and also accompanied him on some of the tours he undertook into the North Indian interior.

Though hampered periodically by illness, Hodges seemed to have toured India in a state of near continual wonder and excitement. Everything impressed him with its unusualness and size, not least the Ganges, which remained until the advent of the railway the main thoroughfare for travellers in India: 'The rivers I have seen in Europe, even the Rhine, appear as rivulets in comparison with this enormous mass of water.' He visited numerous important Hindu and Mughal sites, including the two places that would be most frequently depicted by western artists – Benares and the Taj Mahal. Many Western contemporaries of his also experienced intimations of the Sublime in front of India's monuments; but few of them made as much effort as

he did to view these monuments unprejudiced by the classical canons of architecture. The text he wrote afterwards to accompany his *Select Views in India Drawn on the Spot in the Years 1780, 1781, 1782 and 1783* (London, 1785-8) is one of the most sensitive of the early travel accounts of India, and reveals a tolerance towards an alien culture which was exceptional for his time. He attacked as 'erroneous and servile' the doctrine 'that the Grecian architecture comprizes all that is excellent in art', and thought that architecture 'more than any other art [is] influenced and modified by the nature of the climate and materials, as well as by the habits and pursuits of the inhabitants'.

As someone wholly in sympathy with the scholarly curiosity in Indian monuments shown by contemporaries such as Hastings and Jones, Hodges also strongly believed that an artist's aim in representing these and other exotic works should always be to eschew 'fanciful representation' and to keep the imagination 'under the

Thomas and William Daniell, *Hindu Temple at Brindaram*, 1789; pencil and wash, the British Library Oriental and India Office Collections. This sketch was used for an oil painting which was exhibited at the Royal Academy.

William Daniell, *Thomas and William Daniell viewing Bijaigarh, Uttar Pradesh, from the South-West*, 1790; watercolour, P&O Steam Navigation Company Art Collection. One of the Daniells is sketching whilst the other has interrupted his work to shoot at a passing bird. The need for an awning points to one of the major problems facing *plein air* artists in India.

strict guidance of cool judgement': no matter if an artist was 'possessed of the talents of a Raphael', he would be failing in his artistic duties if he were to eschew the truth, and represent, say, 'a Chinese with the beauty of a Grecian character'. Yet Hodges' own paintings and prints of India contradict his avowed aims, and are composed according to European notions of the Picturesque. He emphasised the loftiness of the monuments he depicted by the use both of foreshortened perspective and of proportions almost as exaggerated as those of David Roberts; and he remained true to the Claudian principles of his teacher Richard Wilson, despite the fact that his early contact with the South Pacific had encouraged a greater spontaneity and freshness in his art. Furthermore images from classical antiquity often came to him –

Thomas and William Daniell, *Old Council House, Calcutta*, 1786-8; pen and wash, the British Library Oriental and India Office Collections. This sketch was used for an oil painting which was exhibited at the Royal Academy.

as they did to Delacroix and other Orientalists – when studying the local people and their exotic costumes. 'To a painter's mind', he wrote after a visit to Benares, 'the fine antique figures never fail to present themselves, when he observes a beautiful female ascending these steps from the river, with wet drapery, which perfectly displays the whole person, and with vases on their heads, carrying water to the temples.'

With his stay in India, which lasted until 1783, Hodges attained the pinnacle of his success as an artist. For over ten years following his return to England, he continued to live off painted and printed views of India, but the quality of his works – according to an early biographer, Edward Edwards – eventually declined owing to 'his desire of appearing as an artist of high rank'. Suffering financially he turned in 1795 from painting to banking, but was bankrupted shortly afterwards, and died a ruined man in 1797.

In the meantime increasing difficulties were being faced by the many artists who followed in Hodges' footsteps to India. The only places in India capable of sustaining large numbers of artists were the Presidency towns of Madras and Calcutta, but there were limits to the amount of patronage available there, and only the most determined or best-connected artists were able to survive. Little help could be expected from the East India Company, which carefully vetted those artists wishing to travel to India, and made them pay a large deposit before embarking on one of their ships. The benefits of using artists to promote Britain's Indian domain were not appreciated by the Company, as was illustrated by their rejection of a proposal made by Thomas Hickey in 1789 to carry out a pictorial survey of India which would emphasise the development of the British as 'imperial rulers of this eastern world'. 'However much', they wrote, 'we wish the promotion of the useful and ingenious arts, the pursuits marked out by Mr. Hickey must be left to the exertions of voluntary enterprise and the encouragement of private patronage.'

The most successful artists to work in India after Hodges were Thomas Daniell and his nephew William. The necessary permission for them to go there had been sought by Thomas from the Company late in 1784, shortly after the latter had issued a statement that no more artists 'should be permitted to proceed to the East Indies this season'. At the time of his application Thomas was a little-known painter, and William his fifteen-year-old apprentice. To improve their chances of being accepted by the Company, Thomas had to claim that he wanted to travel to India as an 'engraver', a medium which had then a shortage of practitioners in Calcutta and Madras. After finally being approved by the Company, they set off to India in the Spring of the following year, but by a most circuitous route. Travellers to India in this period not only had to sail around the Cape of Good Hope, but also were often obliged to go first to China, which was then the main focus of the Company's trading activities and thus served by far more of its boats than was India. The Daniells took the China route, and had to spend a further three months sailing from there to Calcutta, which they finally reached early in 1786. As with all other artists who went to India they would have had to take with them on this long journey all the artist materials they needed: the loss of this equipment would have had disastrous consequences, for almost none of it could be replaced in India itself.

They spent over two years in Calcutta, where they sold numerous engraved views of the city. With the money they earned from these they were able to carry out a plan that had probably been at the back of Thomas's mind from the time he decided to go to India: to tour the Indian interior with the aim of amassing a large collection of drawings that could later be worked up into engravings, oils and finished watercolours. The publication between 1785 and 1788 of Hodges' *Select Views in India* had to a certain extent pre-empted the Daniells' intentions, but they hoped to travel around India more thoroughly than Hodges or any other artist had done. Travelling with limited means on foot, horseback, in small boats, palanquins, and ox-drawn carts, they were to cover thousands of miles and visit areas where no other Europeans had been before. On their first journey they followed in Hodges' footsteps down the Ganges before heading north and becoming the first westerners to visit the Himalayan town of Srinagar. Replenishing their funds with an auction of their

PAGE 63, TOP Thomas and William Daniell, *Near Nobuctu on the Ganges, 23 October 1789*; watercolour, the British Library Oriental and India Office Collections. Despite the exotic details, the handling of the trees and the pastel colouring give this scene an unmistakably English quality.

PAGE 63, BOTTOM Thomas and William Daniell, *The City of Benares*; watercolour, the British Library Oriental and India Office Collections. From the time of William Hodges, the view of Benares from the Ganges became one of the major attractions for artists in India.

RIGHT George Chinnery, *An Indian Hut*; watercolour, the British Library Oriental and India Office Collections. In its freshness of vision and humble subject-matter, Chinnery's art has something in common with that of his English contemporary, Constable.

BELOW James Baillie Fraser, *Gungotree, the Holy Shrine of Mahadeo*, lithograph from *Views in the Himala Mountains*, London, 1802. Fraser was the first artist to provide an extensive pictorial record of the Himalayas.

works in Calcutta, they then went south to Madras, and toured areas of southern India that during the Mysore Wars had been out of bounds to artists. Finally, before returning to England by way of China in 1794, they went by boat to Bombay, from which base they explored with the artist James Wales the then little-known rock-cut temples of western India. At the end of every day's travelling, William would sit down to write up his diary, while Thomas would put the finishing touches to a drawing or two before issuing the servants with plans for the following day. In the course of their extensive travels they collected enough material to enable them, on their return to England, to specialise in Indian scenes for the rest of their lives.

The Daniells, like Hodges before them, insisted on the scientific accuracy of their works, and indeed used a camera obscura while sketching on the spot. Their exploration of uncharted areas of the Himalayas was to be of considerable assistance to the Company's cartographers, while their detailed sketches of buildings were to be used in the late nineteenth century by Lord Curzon when supervising the restoration of India's monuments. Such was the Daniells' concern to emphasise the scientific nature of what they were doing that they denigrated Hodges for being inaccurate. Yet they themselves were as much constrained by the pictorial conventions of their time as was Hodges. Searching always for the Sublime and the Picturesque they generally portrayed broad, variegated and grandiose views, framed these carefully with palms or banjan trees, and, on at least one occasion, enhanced the beauty of a scene with the addition of a temple.

A different and more intimate approach to the Indian environment was shown by George Chinnery, who settled in Madras in 1802 and later moved to Bengal, from where he was forced to flee in 1827 to the island of Macao off the Chinese coast, leaving behind in India both his debts and his wife. Though making a living primarily through painting portraits in oils and miniature, Chinnery's main love appears to have been sketching in close-up the scenes around him. He rejected the sweeping vistas of the Daniells in favour of the more intimate view, and also took a considerable interest in scenes of local life. The only other artist before him to have shown such a fascination with ordinary Indian people had been the Antwerp engraver François Solvyns. Solvyns had taken pains to learn Bengali, but had found it difficult to compete with the British artists, and had enjoyed only a limited success with his *Two Hundred and Fifty Coloured Etchings descriptive of the Manners, Customs and dresses of the Hindoos* (1796-9).

From the time of Chinnery onwards fewer and fewer professional artists undertook the journey to India, the representation of which was left to the hundreds of amateur artists whose works account for nine out of the ten thousand drawings and watercolours kept in London's India House. Among these amateurs were several of Chinnery's pupils, including his devoted patron Sir Charles d'Oyly, and the most intrepid of all the nineteenth-century artists, James Baillie Fraser. Fraser, a lawyer by training, is best known for the pioneering journey he undertook with his brother William in 1815 in search of the sources of the Ganges and Jumna rivers. The foothills of the Himalayas reminded him of his native Scottish Highlands and unleashed what he described as 'The Devil of Drawing'. The drawings that resulted from this burst of creative energy helped, when engraved, to familiarise the British public with one of the least known parts of India.

Another amateur was James Ferguson, who abandoned his directorship of an indigo factory in Calcutta to become one of the leading western experts in Indian architecture. His scholarly writings on this subject were accompanied with impressively detailed drawings that were thought by him to be 'the most correct delineations of Indian architecture that have yet been given to the public'. However, he also admitted that 'in creating of a subject so new and unfamiliar to most people (India), I conceived that the best mode of making it intelligible would be to place a general view of the whole subject before them in a picturesque, and consequently, most understood form'.

As the rift between the British and the Indians widened, the pictorial representation of India acquired an ever more romantic aspect comparable to the exotic distortions of Orientalist painting. William Daniell, though never returning to India, pandered to changing British tastes by producing in the 1830s crowded and sensual scenes filled with bathing beauties and the exotically attired. Other artists, such as the Honourable Emily Eden and John Lewis's much travelled brother

Frederick, concentrated instead on the lavish splendour of Indian court life. Only with the Indian Mutiny of 1857-9 and the appearance of numerous photographs portraying harrowing scenes of famine, poverty and violence, did the reality of Indian life finally impress itself on the British public. The popularity of pictures with Indian subjects began suddenly to wane.

One of the few artists to visit India in the late nineteenth century was Edward Lear, who went there late in life when suffering – together with all his other ailments – from a heart condition. Lear had always harboured a desire to see India, Ceylon and the Himalayas, but an invitation to go there only came in 1871, after his friend Lord Northbrook had been appointed Indian Viceroy. Characteristically turning down the opportunity of travelling to India with the Viceregal suite, Lear set off on his own in October 1872, but found himself stuck at Suez and was unable to 'purSuez eastern journey farther'. He tried again in October of the following year, and, one month later, was finally in Bombay, where he experienced a shock to the system greater than that of any described by artist visitors to North Africa and the Near East. He went, in his own words, 'nearly mad from sheer beauty and wonder of foliage! O new palms!!! O flowers!! O creatures!! O beasts !! . . . anything more overpoweringly amazing cannot be Conceived!!! Colours, & costumes, & myriad-ism of impossible picturesqueness!!!'

Lear would have similar outbursts of enthusiasm at other stages of his Indian journey – for instance, in Benares and in front of the Taj Mahal – but his enjoyment of the country would be tempered by disappointment with the Himalayas, by the exhaustions of constant travel and chaos, and by a distaste for the social niceties of Anglo-Indian life: his stay in the Governor's house in Calcutta was one of the low-points of his tour and led him to describe the city as 'Hustlefussabad'. In spite of all this, however, he managed in the course of thirteen months to travel more extensively around India than almost any artist before him. He covered a vast territory stretching between the Himalayas and Ceylon, and, when he finally sailed home from Bombay in January 1875, he planned a return trip to see all the sights that he had left out.

This trip would not in fact take place, and Lear would spend his last years in his villa at San Remo, never venturing again into the exotic world.

3

The Far East

William Alexander, *Pagoda at Lincing*, watercolour, the British Library Map Room. Like the scene of Chinese barges (see page 75), this is one of a number of finished studies for colour lithographs recording Lord Macartney's embassy to China. It was probably done on the artist's return to England.

Neither India nor any of the Islamic lands favoured by the Orientalists made quite such an impact on western taste as did China and Japan. These two countries represented the ultimate in the exotic, thanks not only to their extreme remoteness, but also to their having been mainly out of bounds to westerners until the mid-nineteenth century. Theirs was an image fostered and maintained by their very inaccessibility, and based hardly at all on direct representations by European artists but instead on a combination of travellers' accounts, and pictures and artefacts by the Chinese and Japanese themselves.

China had not always been closed to foreigners, but had enjoyed a period of lively intercourse with the west during the Han dynasty (206 BC-220 AD), and again during

the so-called Pax Tatarica of the late thirteenth and early fourteenth centuries, when envoys freely travelled between the Pope and Kublai Khan. But more than a century and a half of renewed hostility to foreigners preceded the arrival in China in 1516 of the Portuguese – the first Europeans to sail there since the time of the Romans. A limited trade was sanctioned with the Portuguese, whose help in warding off Chinese pirate ships led in 1557 to their being granted a lease of land on the small peninsular of Macao, which was developed by them as a trading post and is still in their possession today. However, the piratical behaviour of the Portuguese helped to restrict all deeper foreign incursions into the Chinese interior to a few missionaries and members of 'tribute embassies'.

William Alexander, *Chinese Figures from Nature*, 1783; watercolour, the British Library. Alexander was at his best when painting from life. Studies such as these provided the basis for the finished works executed in his English studio.

OPPOSITE William Alexander, *Self-Portrait*; British Museum. The first outstanding western artist to work in China, Alexander was later to become the first director of the British Museum Print Room. He seems to have added the black patch to his face as an afterthought – perhaps so as to enhance his image as an intrepid artist.

Japan was at first far more receptive towards the Portuguese than China, and welcomed the many merchants and missionaries who visited the country in the wake of its 'discovery' in 1543, when two Portuguese adventurers were shipwrecked on the island of Tanegashima. The enormous success of missionaries such as St Francis Xavier in converting the Japanese to Catholicism proved ultimately the undoing of European hopes in Japan, and forced the country in 1638 to cut itself off almost entirely from the West and to allow only the Calvinist Dutch to remain and keep a small trading station on the tiny island of Deijma off Nagasaki.

European trade with the Far East, which had been dominated in the sixteenth century by the Spaniards and Portuguese, came in the course of the following century to be taken over by the Dutch and the British, whose respective East India Trading Companies were founded two years apart. The Dutch began exporting from China shortly after the arrival of their fleet in Canton in 1600; the British had to wait until 1613, after establishing direct contact with Chinese merchants through a base in Siam. Exports, limited initially to silk and spices, were expanded in the seventeenth century to include tea, lacquer and porcelain wares.

Chinese craft objects, with their delicate representations of pagodas, fantastical bridges, winding rivers, craggy peaks, sybaritic courtiers, and exotic flora and fauna, gave substance to western dreams about the mythical land of Cathay described by Marco Polo and other travellers of his generation. A growing fascination with the Far East was reflected from the late sixteenth century in the scholarly researches into China made by such missionaries as the intrepid Jesuit Marco Ricci, who in 1601 went to Peking after spending many years in the Jesuit College at Macao assimilating Chinese language, culture and customs. But the person whose description of China did most to encourage western notions of China in the seventeenth century was Jean Nieuhoff, a steward on the failed Dutch mission of 1644 to try to open normal trade relations with the newly established Manchu dynasty. Nieuhoff described porcelain towers, gilded roof-tops, lacquered interiors, and fantastic rock gardens, and accompanied his account with engravings based on his numerous sketches. These illustrations constituted the earliest important pictorial record made of China by a western artist, and helped fuel the craze for chinoiserie, which swept through Europe during the Baroque and Rococo periods, affecting architecture, design and even philosophy.

Despite this western obsession for things Chinese, it was not until 1793, when this fashion was finally waning, that a professional European artist was to spend any significant amount of time in the Chinese interior. The occasion was a British diplomatic mission which, had it succeeded, might have managed to break down once and for all the barriers between China and the West. Led by Lord Macartney, the mission had as its principal objective the establishment of trade with China on an equal basis, China being hitherto wholly resistant to European imports. Lord Macartney, seeing himself perhaps in the tradition of Enlightenment adventurers such as Cook and Bougainville, thought that his imperialist mission would win much more respect among the Chinese if he brought with him artists or scientists. Though reminded by the President of the East India Company, Lord Dundas, that he 'was not leading a delegation of the Royal Society', he eventually had his way,

LEFT William Alexander, *Seated Chinese Figure*, 1783; watercolour, the British Library. The largest and the boldest of the figure studies which were a result of Alexander's journey to China.

RIGHT William Alexander, *The Fon-yen of Canton when Sitting at Table with the Ambassador in the Hall of the Company's Factory*, 1783; watercolour, the British Library. Alexander was understandably fascinated by the costumes he encountered in China and he later dedicated a book to these.

and secured the service as artists of Thomas Hickey and the twenty-five-year-old William Alexander.

Hickey, who had just returned from an eight-year stay in India, seems to have contributed little to the mission other than play flute accompaniments during the many boring hours of travelling. His nominal deputy Alexander more than made up for Hickey's incompetence by producing an outstanding series of sketches that were later published as coloured lithographs. He also kept a journal which is revealing of the same arrogant, imperialistic attitude towards the Chinese that would lead to the failure of Macartney's mission. As with Macartney, who outraged the Peking court through not kowtowing to the emperor, Alexander refused on one occasion to kneel down in front of a passing mandarin, and felt so smug in his British conscience that he convinced himself that 'this august personnage . . . seemed much amused by my declining this mode of respect'. He found the majority of Chinese women 'had no pretentions to beauty' (his observations on women of 'the middle and superiors orders' were mainly derived from sightings with a telescope), and probably shared the view of his British contemporaries that Chinese artists were technically incom-

petent, being unable to render perspective properly, or to handle shadow and light: no credit appears to have been given to their ability to copy meticulously the various reproductions of European paintings that Macartney had brought with him to China.

On the mission's return to Britain, Hickey was unable to establish himself either in England or in his native Ireland, and so went back to India, where he worked as a portraitist in Madras until his death in 1824. Alexander, meanwhile, though never taking part in any other journey to distant shores, became the illustrator of numerous books of exotic travel, including several on China; in 1808 he was appointed the first director of the British Museum Print Room.

Many of Alexander's British and Dutch contemporaries sketched in the South-East Asian domains of the East India Companies, but most of these artists were amateurs who had acquired their skills during their training as military or engineering officers. The only professionals represented in the large collection of Malaysian and Javanese views amassed in the early nineteenth century by Sir Stamford Raffles were William Westall and William Daniell: the former was merely passing through

William Alexander, *Chinese Barges of Lord Macartney's Embassy*; watercolour, British Museum. Many of the works completed by Alexander on his return to England have a wholly fantastical air.

George Chinnery, *Market Place, Macao*, 1839; pen and ink, British Museum. Chinnery's busy sketches give a great feel of the everyday life of his adopted home.

Malaysia on his way to Australia, while the latter based his illustrations for Raffles' *History of Java* on memories of his long journey to India by way of China. The sole western artist of note to settle in South-East Asia in the early nineteenth century was someone whose very name seemed to predestine him to become a painter of the Far East – George Chinnery.

Though making a name for himself in India, Chinnery is best remembered today for his work in Macao, where he spent the last twenty-seven years of a life that exemplifies the notion of exotic travel as a means of escape. Irish by birth, unstable by temperament, Chinnery had made his first bid for freedom after happily abandoning in Britain his wife, son and daughter so as to come out to India: it was not until fifteen years later that his family were invited to join him there, by which time he had fathered two illegitimate children in Calcutta. His son died of a fever shortly after arriving, while the wife became ever more bitter and petulant. When debts amounting to a staggering forty thousand pounds ('to get so heavily involved

George Chinnery, *Dutch Fort on the Canton River*, 1832; pen and ink, British Museum. Even when sketching a landscape Chinnery preferred close-up views to sweeping vistas.

was a sign of his genius', commented one contemporary) obliged his hasty departure to Macao in 1825, he gleefully took the opportunity to make the definitive break with his wife, whom he once called 'the ugliest woman I ever saw'.

When Chinnery arrived in Macao in September 1825, it was said that he was heading for Canton, where no European woman was allowed to land. The reason for his coming to Macao was probably connected with his friendship with William Jardine, a wealthy Macao-based merchant whom he had met in India and who was to be very influential in getting him the initial contacts on the island. Despite the unappealing aspects of both his personality and his own appearance (a woman sitter described him in the same way as he had described his wife), he apparently also had enormous charm, wit and charisma, which won him immediately the support of the European and Chinese merchant communities. As in India he made a living primarily through portraiture while deriving his greatest pleasure from scenes of local life and landscape, which he sometimes invested with the fanciful picturesqueness of eighteenth-century chinoiserie. Few other artists either before or after him developed such a lazy method of sketching in an exotic setting: every morning his ever more portly body would be carried on a chair by coolies until he reached a motif that interested him, after which he would sit down to work at considerable speed, relishing all the while the astonishment of the large crowds that would inevitably gather round him to watch. Even while remaining resolutely European in his attitude towards life and art, he clearly found in Macao an environment wholly suited to his temperament and ego: he soon gained a large school of followers as well as the nickname 'Artist of the China Coast'.

In 1839, while Chinnery was living in Macao, there broke out the first of the controversial Opium Wars, which would result in Britain gaining both Hong Kong and political domination in South-East Asia; the conflict also brought home the unglamorous reality of modern China, and did away with the last, lingering visions of the fabled Cathay. A taste for Chinese objects remained, but China's role as a catalyst on the western imagination was soon to be usurped by Japan.

For over two centuries after the expulsion of the Jesuits in 1638 Japan had been a virtually unknown country thought vaguely by Europeans to be part of the Chinese Empire and to have a culture no different from that of China. The only information filtering through to the West came from Dutch employees who were obliged to write down their notes in secret and smuggle them out afterwards. The two main western observers of Japan were both doctors, Engelbert Kämpfer and Phillip Franz von Siebold, active respectively in the late seventeenth and early nineteenth centuries. Siebold enjoyed comparative favour in Japan, and, like a number of privileged Europeans before him, was an instructor to highly-placed doctors in Tokyo. He would provide the West with some of its earliest images of Japan through furtively compiling a series of landscape prints: to lessen the danger of being imprisoned as a spy, he commissioned these from native artists. After eight years of living here, he was finally expelled in 1830 after it was revealed that he had persuaded the Court Astronomer to give him a map of the country.

The opening up of Japan occurred with spectacular suddenness during the middle years of the century, and followed on from the forced entry into certain seaports of the British, American, and Russian navies and the consequent signing of an international trade agreement in 1858. Japonaiserie became one of the dominant western fashions of the late nineteenth century, with Japanese prints profoundly influencing the development of European and American painting. When, at the turn of the century, professional artists such as the Scotsman Edward Atkinson Hornel and the Italian Antonio Fontanes finally made their way to Japan, they were able to look at their new environment in a way different from that of earlier artists who had worked in exotic destinations: with eyes as much influenced by the art of the country they were visiting as by the prejudices of western tradition.

4

The South Pacific

OPPOSITE ABOVE Sydney Parkinson, *Vessels of the Island of Otaha, August 1769*; wash, the British Library. A rare example of this scientifically-trained draughtsman attempting meteorological effects.

OPPOSITE BELOW, *A Tupapow in the Island of Otaheite*, 1769; wash, the British Library. The treatment of the trees and background owes something to the works of Claude Lorraine.

The image of the exotic world formed by westerners right up to the beginning of the eighteenth century was based almost entirely on visions of America, North Africa and Asia. The largest ocean of them all, the Pacific, remained largely unexplored, so much so that no one as yet had entirely disproved Ptolemy's assertion of the existence in the southern hemisphere of the *Terra Australis* – a vast continent centred on the Antarctic and thought at one stage to be linked not only to Australia but also to Africa and America.

The Treaty of Tordesillas of 1494 had assigned the southern half of the globe to the Spanish, who persisted for years in establishing a sea-route between Mexico or Peru and the Philippines. Some of the Spanish navigators attempted to look for the legendary *Terra Australis*, and discovered instead the New Hebrides and the Solomon Islands – places that promptly disappeared again from the map owing to a continuing inability to chart positions accurately.

The invention of the chronometer in 1735 entirely transformed the history of navigation, and helped to ensure that by the end of the eighteenth century less than eight per cent of the world's water surface area had still to be explored. The most important of the new navigators was Captain Cook, who initiated the process whereby the world's least-known ocean became the main region outside Europe to be subjected to scientific analysis. He carried out, in the course of his three round-the-world journeys, a thorough scientific study of the flora, fauna, and ethnography of the whole Pacific area; and he had the advantage over land explorers in not having to be sparing in the equipment he could take with him. His vessels, like those of such similar-minded navigators as the great La Perouse, functioned almost as portable laboratories, and, to a certain extent, studios.

With the opening up of the Pacific, artists played a greater role than ever before both in familiarising the western public with exotic lands, and in promoting the advance of Science. Artists had always been a regular feature of scientific missions, but Art and Science had rarely been so closely linked as they were on the voyages of the great Pacific navigators. Professional artists who had been trained in art schools and academies worked alongside scientific and nautical draughtsmen, and were sometimes called upon to do similar work; furthermore they could not help being influenced to some extent by the habits of empirical observation championed both by the Navy and by the British institution which in 1768 had sponsored Cook's first voyage to the South Seas – the Royal Society.

This coming together of Art and Science was not without its tensions and contradictions, as is illustrated in the respective approaches to nature of the Royal

Society and the newly founded institution that was to dominate the training of British artists up to the late nineteenth century – the Royal Academy. Whereas the former exhorted travellers, virtuosi and scientists carefully to record and observe all natural phenomena, the latter preached an idealised view of nature based on classical, Italianate prototype.

The vision of an unspoilt Arcadia that has so often been at the back of western conceptions of exotic lands seemed at first especially appropriate in relation to the South Seas. Louis-Antoine de Bougainville, who reached Tahiti the year before Cook, helped to initiate the myth of the Pacific as a sensual paradise when he described how a bare-breasted Tahitian girl climbed on board his ship, and, slipping off her last vestige of clothing, stood smiling in front of four hundred dumbstruck sailors. 'Like Venus rising from the waves' was how this scene was remembered by Bougainville, who went on to name the place La Nouvelle Cythere after the Peloponnesian island where Aphrodite first emerged from the sea.

The sexual fantasies that such stories as Bougainville's inspired mingled at times with philosophical notions of the 'noble savage': the resulting mixture offered enormous potential to the classically-trained artist, as well as sensual subject-matter comparable to the bath and harem scenes beloved of the Orientalists. However, the spirit of empirical scientific enquiry that was so much a part of the exploration of the Pacific ran counter to the idealisations of artists and philosophers, and, in combination with increasingly bitter confrontations between westerners and 'natives', soon led to the tarnishing of idyllic visions.

One of the most influential of the empirical minds associated with the exploration of the South Seas was Sir Joseph Banks, who accompanied Cook on his first Pacific voyage, and was the person responsible for assembling the *Endeavour*'s team of artists and scientists. A future President of the Royal Society, as well as a member of the Society of Dilettanti, and of the Society of Arts (an institution dedicated to further the links between art, science and technology), Banks was a supreme 'virtuoso' whose early interest in archaeology was supplanted by an obsession with botany and exotic animals. As for the visual arts, his vision was rather more limited, and he was wholly out of sympathy with the views of the Royal Academy and its president Sir Joshua Reynolds. The artist Joseph Farrington summarised Banks's straightforward artistic tastes when he wrote that 'Accuracy of drawing seems to be a principal recommendation to Sir Joseph.'

Banks could hardly have been looking for little else in the two artists whom he chose to take with him on the *Endeavour*. One of these was Sydney Parkinson, who was originally employed merely to execute scientific illustrations of plants and animals; the other was Alexander Buchan, an obscure topographical artist whom Banks had envisaged as producing a record of both the landscapes and peoples seen on the voyage. Buchan's few surviving works include a representation of a group of Tierra del Fuegans huddled together in their hut, a work which would later be transformed in the engraved version (by Bartolozzi after Cipriani) featured in Hawkesworth's best-selling account of the *Voyages*: in the engraving, Buchan's crude and stumpy figures have been given a classical grace and poise, while the hut itself has been lent the noble simplicity of Langier's famous illustration of the *Origins of*

OPPOSITE Sydney Parkinson, *Portrait of a New Zealand Man*, *c.*1769; pen and wash, the British Library. Parkinson recorded the natives of the South Pacific with the scientific detachment of an anthropologist.

Architecture. The artistic licence of the engraving angered at least one scientist of the time, and would certainly have met with the disapproval of Banks, whose admiration for Buchan's faithfulness to his subject made him probably turn a blind eye to his obvious limitations as a figure painter. Sadly, Buchan, an epileptic, was not to have much opportunity to improve his skills, for he died of a fit shortly after reaching Tasmania. Banks was distraught, though not entirely for humanitarian reasons. 'His loss to me is irretrievable', he wrote in a revealing entry in his Journal, 'my airy dreams of entertaining my friends in England with the scenes I am to see here have vanished.'

Banks's worries on this score were unfounded, for after Buchan's death his duties as an artist were ably assumed by Sydney Parkinson, some of whose views even reveal an interest in the depiction of atmospheric and climatic conditions that looks ahead to the Pacific landscapes of William Hodges. Parkinson was also adept at what must have been the most difficult task facing any of the explorer artists: the portrayal of the indigenous populations. Fortunately he seems to have possessed, like Cook and Hodges, an ability to establish friendly contact with the natives – an essential asset for anyone wishing to persuade them to pose for a sketch. Moreover, his interest in these peoples had none of the sexual element of that of Cook's sailors, and it also extended to a fascination with their languages, the words of which he conscientiously attempted to write down. What is lacking in Parkinson's unidealised representations of native peoples is any real human dimension, his approach remaining always that of the ethnographer who observes expressions and costumes in the same detached manner that the botanist approaches plants. The talents of a William Hodges were needed to achieve what neither of Banks's two artists had been able to do – the reconciliation of Art and Science.

Hodges' first opportunity to work in an exotic climate came shortly after the return of the *Endeavour* to England in 1771. Cook's first voyage, and Banks's contribution towards it, had been considered an enormous success, but there was still concern that the question of the existence of a vast southern continent had yet to be fully resolved. With this in mind Cook planned a second round-the-world voyage in 1772, and once again Banks set about gathering a scientific and artistic team to accompany it. This time the artistic party he had in mind was both larger and stronger than before, comprising as it did two natural history draughtsmen, one marine painter, and Johann Zoffany, one of the most accomplished portraitists and genre-painters of his age. However, Banks was soon to withdraw both his support and that of the Royal Society after claiming that the cabins of Cook's new ship, the *Resolution*, were too small for the needs of his team. Thanks to Banks, the presence of such a team was now deemed so essential to the success of a voyage of discovery that the Admiralty immediately began to form a replacement one. Instead of Zoffany there was chosen his young and barely tested artist friend William Hodges, who, in the absence of Banks, was to take his orders directly from Captain Cook himself.

Hodges' exceptional openness to new environments and cultures, his questioning of the supremecy of classical prototypes, and his concern for representing the unadorned truth, have already been noted in relation to his Indian pictures (see pages 60-64). These qualities – almost certainly acquired as a result of working with

Cook and the scientists of the *Resolution* – would always be in conflict with the Claudian, Picturesque principles demanded of the landscape artists of his age. However, in the course of his long journey to the South Seas, he was to allow himself a greater spontaneity than at any other stage of his life. The resulting works include some of the finest pictures ever painted by an artist in an exotic climate, and have a freshness and originality that would rarely be recaptured in British landscape art up to the time of Constable.

Alone among Richard Wilson's distinguished pupils, and indeed unlike most other ambitious British artists of the eighteenth century, Hodges never completed his artistic education in Italy. He did so instead in the South Seas, where he could give free rein to his more experimental tendencies. His freedom from the academic practices of the time was evident above all in his espousal of plein-air oil painting, a practice encouraged by Wilson, but employed by Hodges to a greater extent than any previous artist (he seems, moreover, to have been the first painter to have worked regularly in oils on an exotic journey). The term *plein-air* is in fact a misnomer, as the magnificent landscape oils resulting from his trip were probably all painted from the large window of Cook's cabin. Working under such conditions had the advantage of privacy and security, and was often essential when moored in a foreign port such as Cape Town, where anyone caught sketching was likely to be thought of as a spy making a record of defensive systems; the shape of the cabin window provided also a natural frame enabling Hodges to single out more easily landscape motifs. From the comfort and cosiness of the cabin Hodges was able to observe with an almost scientific detachment all manner of landscapes and weather effects; and, as the journey progressed, he was able to do so with an ever increasing facility, so that the stiff and static nature of some of his earlier compositions gave way in the South Seas to effortless and magically luminous landscapes that capture for the first time in art the brilliance of light in the tropics.

The Pacific landscapes that Hodges executed on his return to England inevitably lacked the freshness of the ones done *in situ*; but they were also composed in a way that would appeal more to the tastes of the time, and thus ensure a greater commercial viability. One of the finer examples is the so-called *Tahiti Revisited*, in which details of botanical and ethnographic interest (such as the accurately rendered banana trees, and tattoo patterns) are absorbed in a grandiose Claude-like composition with dramatically-posed foreground figures of classical inspiration.

Though landscapes were Hodges' primary interest, he also made on the voyage numerous sketches of local peoples that differ from those of Buchan and Parkinson not just in treating their subjects as ethnographic types but in rendering character and expression as well. An anecdote related by one of the *Resolution*'s scientists, Anders Sparrman, highlights the particular problems faced by Hodges when wanting to realise one such portrait. A young Maori woman, handsomely paid by him to come and pose in the ship's saloon, 'imagined that she ought to give satisfaction, in the way she understood it', presumably on the basis of previous encounters with sailors. When she realised, however, that all she had to do was to sit on a chair, she was totally astounded, and was later overcome with 'wonderment and entertainment' the moment 'she saw her likeness in a red chalk drawing'.

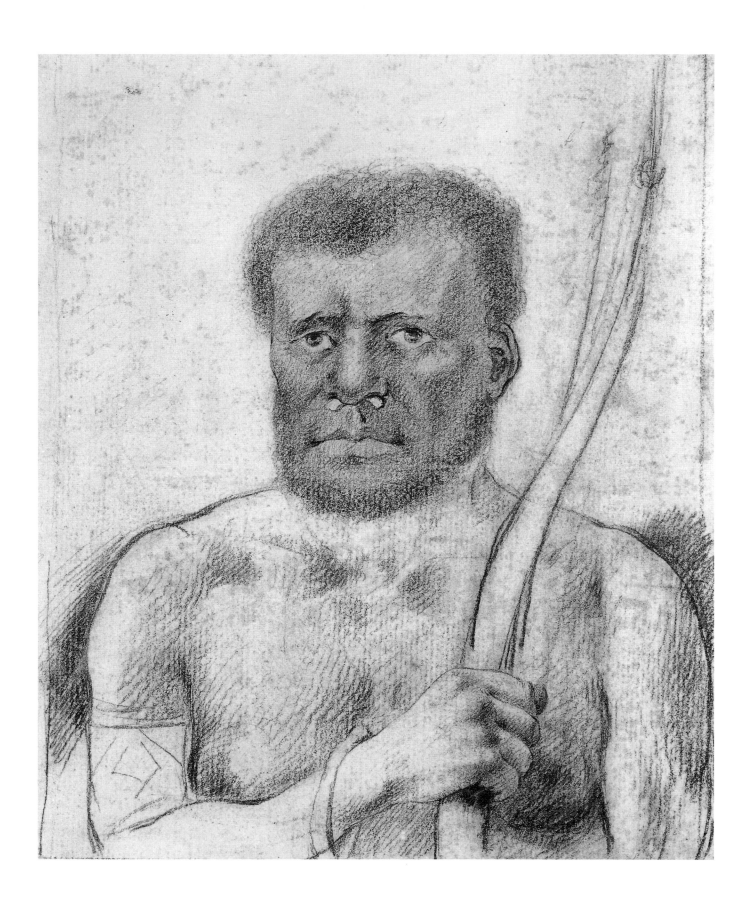

John Webber, *A Dance at Otaheite*, 1777;
wash, the British Library. One of Webber's
many records of the entertainments put on
for Cook by tribal elders.

The recording of indigenous people seems to have become an increasingly important part of the artistic programme of Cook's voyages. On the third voyage, undertaken with the main purpose of discovering a northern sea passage between the Atlantic and Pacific, the appointed artist was John Webber, an artist of Swiss descent who seems to have been hurriedly chosen on the basis of a portrait he exhibited at the Royal Academy in 1776. By this date, the success of Hawkesworth's illustrated editions of Cook's travels had been so great that the accompanying artist was now expected not just to depict faithfully what he saw but also to produce works that would popularise the voyage. 'To make the result of our voyage entertaining to the generality of readers', wrote Cook,

as well as instructive to the sailor and scholar, Mr. Webber was pitched upon, and engaged to embark with me, for the express purpose of supplying the unavoidable imperfections of written accounts, by enabling us to preserve and bring home, such drawings of the most memorable scenes of our transactions, as could be executed by a professed and skilful artist.

Webber was a prolific artist who produced perhaps the most comprehensive record of all the voyages – a record, moreover, which corresponds very closely to Cook's written descriptions. His energies were channelled principally into the creation of large watercolours celebrating each of Cook's major landfalls, and usually depicting either Cook's first encounter with the local people, or else the entertainments put on for him by the tribal elders. These watercolours, featuring appropriate and closely observed landscape backgrounds, incorporated numerous sketches made by Webber while Cook's men were engaged in the customary bartering and collecting of wood and water. Despite their pretensions to documentary and scientific accuracy, these works were given a self-consciously artistic quality through Webber's mannered and elongated figures, which were possibly intended to enhance the dignity of the indigenous peoples.

Webber's truthfulness as an artist was also lessened by certain restrictions and obligations imposed on him by Cook. The censures of the Methodist clergy, together

John Webber, *A Human Sacrifice at Otaheite*, 1777; watercolour, the British Library. Captain Cook and his men display their civilised, European values by removing their hats at this scene of impending barbarity.

with the many ribald jokes appearing in the British press about the sexual availability of the South Sea Islanders, made Cook wary of promoting too sensual an image of the South Pacific. Additionally, in view of colonial ambitions in the South Seas, he was keen not to show the local peoples in too savage and violent a light. Not least, he had developed by this stage in his life such an obsession with his own image that Webber had to act partly as his hagiographer, and to show him in the role of bringer of peace and prosperity.

Cook's increasingly touchy and irrational behaviour on his third voyage must have made Webber's task of showing him and his mission in positive, heroic terms an ever more difficult one. Cook, who had displayed so much common sense, patience and understanding on his earlier voyages, was now in danger of losing the respect of the locals through resorting to cruel and violent punishments that were wholly inappropriate to someone supposedly civilising the South Pacific. His new irascibility has been blamed on illness, but it was probably also connected with his sad realisation that the South Seas was no longer the paradise he had originally thought, and that he and other Europeans had themselves managed in a short space of time to corrupt it through introducing such western ills as syphilis and a market economy. It was perhaps fitting that this should have been his last voyage, and that he should have met his death at the hands of the South Sea Islanders, with whom he had once tried so hard to establish good relations. Whether or not Webber himself had been present at the famous skirmish at the Sandwich Island of Owhyhee, it was his representation of the event (engraved by Bartolozzi) which was to provide the final memorable image of Cook – a heroic image with Cook's arm outstretched in a classical pose suggesting both bravery and a last bid for peace.

After the death of Cook, the navigation of the Pacific was dominated by French officers, beginning with La Pérouse, who set off to the South Seas in 1785 on a scientific mission directly inspired by the official account of Cook's third voyage. A special emphasis of this trip was on the study of the local peoples, whose artefacts were systematically collected for the first time. Instructions more detailed than those ever delivered to Cook's artists were given to the mission's landscape and figure-draughtsman, Duché de Vancy, who, with the assistance of two natural history draughtsmen, the Prevosts, was asked to prepare 'portraits of the natives of the different parts, their dresses, ceremonies, buildings, boats and vessels, and all the productions of the sea and land . . . if he shall think that drawings of them will render the descriptions more intelligible'.

As most of these drawings were lost when La Pérouse perished and his vessels were destroyed on the coral reefs of Vanikoro, the main visual record of the journey are the decidedly unscientific engravings published in the *Atlas du Voyage de La Pérouse* (1797). Though lacking the anthropological accuracy demanded of the artists, these illustrations are an interesting reflection of changing attitudes towards the inhabitants of the Pacific: one of the plates, of Easter Island, combines a classical idealisation of the natives with details showing them stealing from members of La Pérouse's crew. La Pérouse himself developed an ever more hostile attitude towards the people encountered on his journey, and, for the first of many times in the literature on the Pacific, contrasted the beauty and arcadian luxurance of its islands

OPPOSITE John Webber, *The Plantain Tree in the Island of Cracatoa*; watercolour, British Museum. Though best known for his figurative studies, Webber was also able at times to capture the beauty of the exotic landscape, as in this sketch for an aquatint reproduced in *Views of the South Seas*, 1808.

John Webber, *The Death of Captain Cook*; oil on canvas, Dixson Galleries, State Library of New South Wales. A painted version of Webber's often reproduced engraving of the same subject; Cook's heroic pose is derived from classical reliefs of battle scenes.

with the savagery and deceit of those who lived there. Any lingering notions of the 'noble savage' were dispelled for him once and for all after the massacre at Samoa of twelve of his companions, a scene in which – in the engraved version – the extreme violence is only partially mitigated by the suggestion of an idyll conveyed by the presence of classical-style nude women and children under a palm tree.

Two of the most important groups of illustrations resulting from South Seas voyages in the wake of Cook were those produced on the scientific expeditions led respectively by Nicolas Baudin and Matthew Flinders in the first years of the nineteenth century. The scientific contingent travelling with Baudin on the *Géographe* and the *Naturaliste* was an especially large one consisting of five zoologists, five gardeners, four artists, four astronomers and hydrographers, three botanists and two mineralogists. However, thanks to Baudin's incompetence and lack of sympathy with the scientists, many of this team, including three of the artists, left the

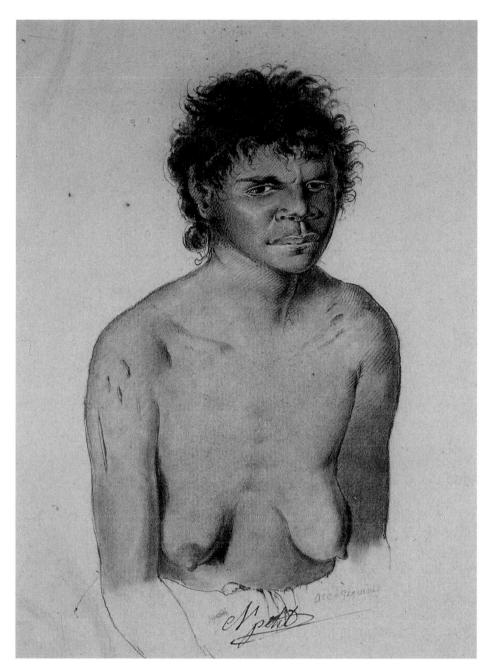

Nicolas-Martin Petit, *A Young Australian Aboriginal Woman*, inscribed 'Oie-requine', *c*.1801-3; pastel, Museum d'Histoire Naturelle, Le Havre. Petit's drawings of the peoples of the South Pacific achieve at times a naturalism comparable to Lesueur's animal studies.

BELOW Charles-Alexandre Lesueur, *Dasurus viverrinus* (Quall: a native Australian cat), *c*.1801-3; gouache on vellum, Museum d'Histoire Naturelle, Le Havre. On Lesueur's return to France a scientific committee deemed his 1500 or so detailed drawings and paintings of animals 'the most complete and the most precious series of the kind that we have any knowledge of . . .'.

expedition at Mauritius. The task of recording the voyage was left in consequence to an obscure portrait-painter called Nicolas Petit, and to someone who had joined the expedition in the humble capacity of apprentice helmsman but whose brilliance at natural history illustration was soon recognised – Charles-Alexandre Lesueur. While some of Petit's portrayals of Tasmanians and Australian Aborigines have an uncannily lifelike naturalism, the works of Lesueur broke new ground in the development of what has been called the 'typical landscape' – a type of landscape in which Neo-classical and picturesque notions of mood and expression have been succeeded by the more scientific concern of placing plants, animals and primitive peoples in their natural habitat.

Matthew Flinders' expedition of 1800-3 was a much smaller affair than Baudin's, but had the distinction of being the first to circumnavigate the Australian coast; it was also thanks to Flinders that the territory now recognised as the fifth continent was given the name of the mythical land mass mentioned by Ptolemy. Enjoying as it did the support of Sir Joseph Banks, Flinders' expedition had a strong botanical bias, and benefited from the presence of the botanist Robert Brown, whose study of

his Australian findings (*Prodromus Florae Novae Hollandiae*) was described by his eminent colleague Joseph Dalton Hooker as 'the greatest botanical work that has ever appeared'. No less impressive than the text were the book's illustrations, which were by the expedition's botanical draughtsman, Ferdinand Bauer, an artist whose ability to reveal in his plant and animal drawings both beauty and scientific structure seems to account for the great esteem in which he was held by Goethe.

Something of the scientific meticulousness of Bauer seems to have rubbed off on the expedition's appointed landscape painter, William Westall, who was chosen as a substitute to William Daniell after the latter had become engaged to Westall's sister. Much of his work for Flinders involved the making of coastal profiles so detailed as to be of enormous use to navigators. But though he invested these technical drawings with considerable beauty and atmosphere, his principal intention in visiting the South Seas was not to further scientific and nautical studies, but rather to search out the exotic – an impulse increasingly common among artist travellers of the Romantic era, and one that would lead him immediately afterwards to China and India. The barren and monotonous coastline of much of Australia, however, did not live up

William Westall, *View of Sir Edward Pellew's Group, Gulf of Carpentaria*, 1812; oil on canvas, Admiralty House, London. This atmospheric painting is a departure from Westall's many laborious coastal profiles.

Augustus Earle *Solitude – Watching the Horizon at Sunset, in the Hopes of Seeing a Vessel – Tristan de Acunha, in the South Atlantic*, 1824; watercolour, National Library of Australia, Canberra. Earle's main companion here during his many months of waiting for a boat was his faithful dog, Jemmy.

to his exotic expectations. 'I was not aware', he wrote to Banks soon after leaving Flinders' ship, 'the voyage was confined to New Holland only had I know this I most certainly would not have engaged in a hazardous voyage where I could have little opportunity of employing my pencil with any advantage to myself or my employers.'

An appreciation of the Australian landscape took a long time to develop, and was cultivated more by artist settlers than by artist travellers. Some of the earliest Australian landscapists were convicts, many of whom had once put their artistic talents to the forging of bank-notes. One such artist was Joseph Lycett, who used eighteenth-century pictorial devices to describe the Australian scene, and who showed little understanding of such intrinsic features of the landscape as the harshness of the light and colour, and the sparseness of the bush. A contemporary of his, Judge Barron Field, emphasised the European preference for tightly grouped trees when he wrote that 'New South Wales is a perpetual flower garden, but there is not a single scene in it of which a painter could make a landscape without greatly disguising the character of the trees. They have no lateral boughs and cast no masses of shade.' These perceived failings of the Australian landscape were also disguised by the greatest artist to have worked here in the early years of the century, Charles Glover, who settled with his family in Tasmania at the age of sixty-three, and persistently rendered the scenery in terms of a Claudian pastoral idyll.

Much of the Australian interior was of course still unknown at this time, and skills other than painting were needed for those who travelled much beyond the coast. Appropriately, as with America, surveyors played a major role in the early history of Australian landscape art. Thomas Livingstone Mitchell, a Scottish settler in charge of the Australian Ordnance Survey, had a particularly strong influence; in his panoramic drawings executed in the course of four expeditions through New South Wales between 1831 and 1846, he conveyed the unexpected beauty and fertility of large parts of the virgin interior. 'Of this Eden', he wrote,

it seemed that I was only the Adam; and it was indeed a sort of paradise to me, permitted thus to be the first to explore its mountains and streams – to behold its scenery – to investigate its geological character – and, finally, by my survey, to develop those natural advantages still unknown to the civilized world, but yet certain to become important to a new people.

Whereas someone like Mitchell could look at a natural wilderness with a view to scientific survey and future colonisation, artist travellers of the romantic era were often more interested in novel, exotic sensations. The most colourful of the artist travellers to have worked in the South Seas was perhaps Augustus Earle, the eccentric Englishman whose quite exceptional restlessness earned him the nick-name of the 'the wandering artist'. A passion for novelty and adventure was revealed when, on a visit to Tristan da Cunha in 1824, he described his excitement on going off with his 'dog, gun, boat cloak and sketchbook' to work in a 'spot hitherto unvisited by the artist'. Unfortunately, this particular adventure led him to spend rather more time on the island than he had intended, for he returned to his boat only to find it sailing away. The next boat out did not arrive until six months later, and, instead of taking him to South America, his original destination, sidetracked him to the South Pacific.

Deeply romantic in his approach towards nature, Earle was to display in the South Seas an interest in the native peoples which had little to do with ethnography. This interest led him, in New Zealand, to take up a 'temporary residence among the natives in the hope of finding something new for my pencil in their peculiar and picturesque style of life'. Though he came expecting to witness all manner of barbaric practices, he ended up forgiving the Maoris' 'many defects' and forming a genuine respect for them. None the less, in criticising the Missionaries for attempting to civilise the Maoris, he was not just expressing this respect but also holding on to an inherently romantic vision of a people whose nakedness brought to mind the heroic beauty of ancient Rome and Greece. That his attitude towards distant lands was essentially romantic and unscientific is finally confirmed in his famous canvas of a *Waterfall in Australia* (c. 1826), in which the sketching artist is portrayed as if directly under the inspiration of the naked aborigine who looms up behind him like some exotic variant of a classical muse.

Augustus Earle, *Waterfall in Australia*,
*c.*1826; oil on canvas, National Library of
Australia, Canberra. The artist is depicted
sketching in the foreground.

5

America

In the wake of Columbus's journey to what he imagined as the East, European artists began at last to furnish the western world with a wide-ranging visual record of exotic lands. So much new ethnographic, anthropological, zoological and botanical material was now coming to light that the mere accounts of travellers were no longer sufficient to satisfy western interest in these novelties. However, for most of the early history of the exploration and colonial development of the New World, written testimonies easily outnumbered visual ones: interestingly, the Council of Indies in Seville made no mention of drawings when requesting its officials for detailed information on the customs and natural history of their territories.

Few professional artists visited America before the eighteenth century, and even fewer of these displayed the degree of skill achieved by the Renaissance artist in the objective portrayal of the natural world. Moreover, very little of the early visual material relating to America was actually done there: most of it, instead, was either executed from memory on the artist's return to Europe, freely engraved from now-lost field sketches, or else fuelled by such fantasies as Raleigh's tale about Venezuela's headless men with eyes in their shoulders.

It is particularly surprising – given both the Renaissance interest in the study of man, and the degree of realism attained in European portraiture of the time – how few artists responded initially to the challenge of creating accurate likenesses of the hundreds of new peoples with whom westerners came into contact after 1492. Only 268 representations of native Americans are known from before 1590, and in virtually all of these the subjects have been given European features. Gonzalo Fernandez de Oviedo, in his *Natural y general historia de las Indias* (1535-7) recognised that pictures were potentially far more capable than words of giving westerners some idea of what America's indigenous population was like; however, he also emphasised that such works would have to be by artists of the stature of a Leonardo da Vinci, a Mantegna, or a Berruguete (a Spanish Renaissance painter active in Italy), and that in any case neither pictures nor words could replace the experience of seeing the New World with one's own eyes.

The same conclusion was reached in Jean de Léry's *Histoire d'un voyage fait en la terre du Brésil* (1578), which, in addition, elaborates on the difficulties that Europeans had in portraying native Americans. 'Although', de Léry wrote,

I diligently perceived and remarked those barbarian people, for a whole year together, wherein I lived amongst them, so as I might conceive in my mind a certain idea or proportion of them, yet I say, by reason of their diverse gestures and behaviour, utterly different from ours, it is a very difficult matter to express their true proportion, either in writing or in painting: but if anyone covets to enjoy the full pleasure of them, I could wish with him to go into America himself.

The earliest artist known to have gone to America was Jacques Le Moyne, a Huguenot who was born in 1533 in Dieppe. He was probably trained in the town's famous schools of manuscript illumination and cartography, but nothing is documented about his life until 1564, when he took part in the French attempt to colonise Florida – an attempt supported by Charles IX of France and intended both to challenge Spanish claims to the southern regions of North America, and to establish a settlement where Huguenots could live free from persecution. The expedition he joined, under the command of Laudonnière, would prove almost as much of a failure as the one led two years earlier by Jean Ribaut. Dissension among its members was followed by a devastating attack by the Spanish, in the course of which Le Moyne witnessed from a hiding-place the brutal killing of many of his companions. After escaping across perilous swamps, he managed to get back to France, only to arrive there in the tense years preceding 1572. He ended his days in England, where he was welcomed by Raleigh, who probably introduced him to that other pioneering artist traveller – John White.

In the account that Charles IX encouraged him to write of his American experiences, Le Moyne recorded that it was his 'special duty when we reached the Indies . . . to map the sea coast, and lay down the position of towns, the depth and course of rivers and the harbours; and to represent also the dwellings of the natives, and whatever in the province might seem worthy of observation.'

Among Le Moyne's surviving original works, which were not discovered until after 1900, are some watercolours of exotic fruits and flowers, and a painting on vellum of one of the scenes later engraved for the illustrated edition of his American travels. This painting, showing a column erected by Ribaut in 1562 to mark French sovereignty in Florida, features Laudonnière in the company of the Timacuan Indian chief Athore, who has inspired his tribesmen to worship and lay down offerings in front of the marker column. Recent archaeological evidence has shown that the pendants hanging from Athore's belt, and the two votive basins beside him are closely based on real Timacuan objects. Other details, such as the wicker baskets and the fruits within them are probably derived from European prototypes, while the gilding and bright colouring of the tattoos reflect more on the conventions of manuscript illumination than on genuine Indian tattoos. The Timacuans themselves look less European than they do in the engravings after Le Moyne, but they have been given a suitable docility and malleability in accordance with the artist's propaganda intentions. One of the earliest representations by a travelling artist of a 'savage people', this work sets the tone for many more to come in the way in which its ethnographic value is undermined by its wholly European mode of seeing and understanding.

The engraved versions of Le Moyne's illustrations were commissioned by the Protestant Frankfurt publisher De Bry, who, after the artist's death, managed also to persuade his widow to sell him all her late husband's drawings of Florida. Once

Jacques Le Moyne, *René de Laudonnière and Chief Athore*, 1564; gouache, Print Collection, The New York Public Library. The column in the background, erected by the French several years before Laudonnière's expedition, is here shown as an object of local veneration so as to emphasise the ease with which the French were colonising the New World. Ironically it would be pulled down shortly afterwards by the Spanish.

engraved, Le Moyne's originals seem to have lost all value for De Bry, who probably allowed them to be destroyed – a telling indication of the low artistic esteem in which the early artist travellers were held. However, the potential widespread interest in Le Moyne's subject-matter was immediately recognised by such a brilliant entrepreneur as De Bry, who, after popularising Le Moyne, would go on to plan editions in four languages of engravings after John White. Neither De Bry nor his engravers ever went to America, and, in the absence of field sketches, filled out exotic depictions by conflating material from different sources, including European ones. Renaissance Italian works, such as Pollaiuolo's *Battle of the Naked Men* and Michelangelo's *Battle of Cascina*, influenced the compositions and facial types, and helped to strengthen the nobility of the Indians, who are always shown in favourable contrast to the brutal Spanish.

The manner of their fishing.

The Spanish who went to the New World were not of course just the ruthless conquerors portrayed by such Protestant perpetuators of Spain's 'Black Legend' as Le Moyne and De Bry. It was in fact the Spanish king, Philip II, who instigated what was probably the first scientific expedition to an exotic destination. Led by the physician Francisco Hernández, it toured Mexico between 1571 and 1576, and amassed in the process no less than fifteen volumes of descriptions and illustrations of plants and animals. Unpublished in the sixteenth century, and thus very limited in the scope of their influence, these volumes were lost in 1671 in a fire at the Escorial which also destroyed a series of decorative paintings in Philip's antechamber that were inspired by some of the illustrations.

The British adventurer Richard Hakluyt the elder, writing about transatlantic voyages in the early 1580s, listed among the people who should form part of a ship's crew, 'a skilful painter . . . which the Spaniards used commonly in all their discoveries to bring the descriptions of all beasts, birds, fishes, trees, townes, etc.' In 1585-6, Sir Francis Drake recruited a Portuguese artist, Baptiste Boazio, to accompany him on a tour of the West Indies. But, after Le Moyne, the only other sixteenth-century artist visitor to the New World whose works have survived was the English Protestant, John White.

The early life of John White is as little known as that of Le Moyne. Born *c*.1540-50, and married in the late 1560s, he is probably to be identified with the John White mentioned in 1580 as a member of the Painter-Stainer's Company. Looking back on his life in 1593, White referred to five journeys across the Atlantic, the earliest of which might well have been with Martin Frobisher, who, between 1576 and 1578 made the first serious attempt to discover a north-west route to Asia, and, in so doing, brought westerners into contact for the first time with Eskimos. The evidence for White's presence on this expedition are some Eskimo sketches attributed to him, one of which depicts a skirmish with Frobisher's men.

The most important and best documented period in White's life was when he participated in Raleigh's three attempts to establish an English colony in Virginia – an initiative constituting the first serious English efforts to examine and settle North America. Between 1584 and 1586, White's role in this mission was a subordinate one which, in addition to his duties as artist-observer, possibly included the assisting of the pilots in the making of coastal profiles and sea-charts, and such administrative jobs as that of purser; but from 1587 onwards he became the principal agent in charge of the venture.

A preliminary reconnoitre of the North American coast in 1584 was followed a year later by a more thorough expedition to the newly named Virginia. On this second voyage, led by Sir Richard Grenville, a stop was made at Hispaniola, where, according to the Spaniards, the Englishmen 'took away with them many banana plants and other fruit-trees which they found along the shore, and made drawings of fruits and trees'. White was also named as one of those who rowed across Pamlico Sound from the island of Wococon to accompany Grenville on a visit to a number of Indian villages on what is now the South Carolina mainland.

Working closely with White on this trip was the brilliant mathematician, cartographer and ethnologist Thomas Hariot, whose *Briefe and true report of the new found land of Virginia* offers much insight into his partnership with White, and shows how the theoretical knowledge of the former was complemented by the latter's practical skills. When they were engaged on cartographical work, they would either carry out a systematic survey of an area, or else – if they had less time to spare – make rough sketches from which maps were later compiled. When it came to plants and wildlife, specimens were taken wherever possible, and meticulous notes were made by Hariot to illuminate White's sketches. 'We have taken', wrote Hariot, 'eaten, and have the pictures as they were then drawne of the inhabitants of several strange sorts of water foule eighte and seventeen kinds more of land foule.' The most fruitful outcome of the two men's collaboration resulted from Hariot's special responsibility to discover as much as possible about the Indians, a task that led White to carry out a fascinating record of the inhabitants and customs of the villages that they got to know best.

White returned to England with a substantial body of sketches that he then began to use as the basis for his finished drawings. However, art was no longer foremost in his mind, for, unlike many others of those who had gone with him to Virginia, he had come back from America with an enormous enthusiasm for what he had seen, and a determination to encourage people to go and settle there. He himself took on the job of recruitment, and was duly appointed captain of the boat that would carry the new colonists to Virginia. Through the offer of 500 acres of land to each prospective colonist, White had hoped to bring with him at least 150 people, but in the end only 84 men, 17 women and 11 children came along. Among those who set off for Virginia in 1587 were his daughter and son in law, Eleanor and Ananias Dare, whose future child would be the first English one to be born in America.

As a captain White proved rather less competent than he was as a draughtsman, and he appeared to have great difficulty in exerting any control over the ship's master, Simon Fernandez. The original intention was to make their way to Chesapeake Bay after picking up a number of settlers who had been left behind by Grenville at the Virginian island of Roanoke; but they were to remain at Roanoke on the insistence of Fernandez, who might possibly have feared Indians at Chesapeake Bay, but more likely was acting out of sheer bloody-mindedness. After a short while on the island White was elected to return to England for supplies. Delayed by the Spanish Armada and by an attack by a French vessel, White finally got back to Roanoke to find the settlement abandoned and his possessions left to ruin. Some of the settlers had apparently moved on to the island of Croatoan, but most had probably perished, possibly at the hands of the Indians. His idyllic vision of life in America destroyed, White went back once more to England, where nothing more is heard of him after 1590.

Great claims have been made for White as an artist, though it is unlikely that much attention would be paid to his work were it not for the fascination and scientific value of its subject-matter. Of great importance to the historian of cartography, his work also constitutes one of the finest early records of exotic flora, fauna, and wildlife. But, above all, it is of enormous enthnographic and an- thropological significance, and, in combination with Hariot's texts, provides the sole literate record of the disappeared Algonkian Indians of South Carolina. White's

John White, *Loggerhead Turtle*; watercolour, British Museum. The first known copy of White's work was of this drawing.

RIGHT John White, *Flying Fish*; watercolour, British Museum. Not always successful in his use of perspective, White has rendered here the top and side impressions of the fish in the same drawing.

BOLADORA

One of the wyues of Wyngyno.

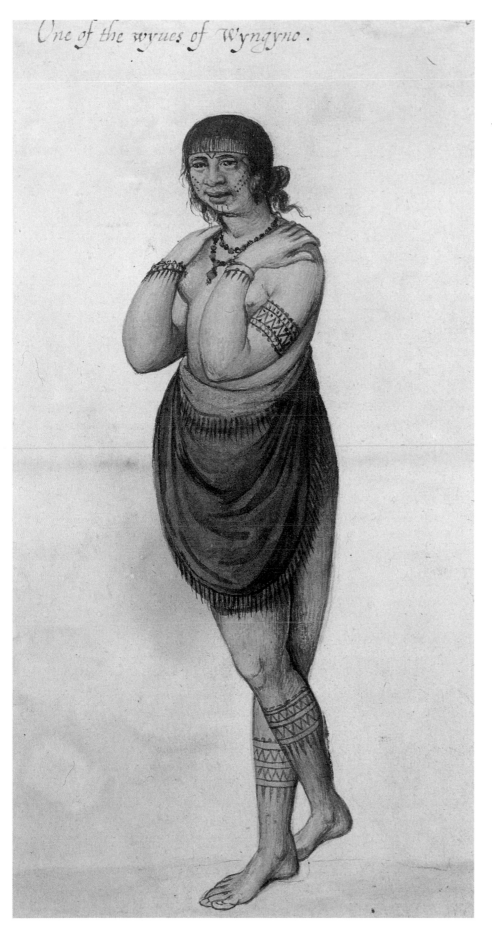

John White, *Indian Woman*; watercolour, British Museum. White, not the greatest of technical masters, has given the woman two right feet – one of the problems, perhaps, of drawing from memory.

drawings of Indians, and of their customs and dwellings, have a far more authentic and less European look than those of Le Moyne and De Bry, and, through depicting such perishable features of Algonkian culture as their objects made from wood, bark, fur, leather, and feathers, supply the type of data that archaeology cannot do. However, White's finished drawings cannot be claimed as wholly objective portrayals. In the case of the one called *The Flyer*, the Indian's pose has been made to emulate a statue of *Mercury* by the highly refined Italian sculptor Giambologna. And throughout, in accordance with White's hopes of attracting English settlers, the Indians are shown as peaceful, home-loving people who do not go round in the state of shameless nudity described by others.

It is certainly difficult to imagine how a European public used to such ultimately quaint and artificial representations of America by the likes of Le Moyne, De Bry, and even White would have reacted to the works of the next two important artists to have worked in America – Frans Post and Albert Eckhout. The first painters of outstanding quality to portray the exotic world, these two Dutch visitors to seventeenth-century Brazil rendered the American scene with a naturalism that few other travelling artists would achieve before the nineteenth century.

Post and Eckhout travelled to Brazil in the retinue of the illustrious Dutch soldier and statesman, Count Johann Maurits of Nassau-Siegen, who, from 1637 to 1644, was Governor of the colony that the Dutch West India Company briefly established in the north-eastern part of the country. The Dutch, ever since gaining their independence from Spain in the early seventeenth century, had emerged as the world's dominant sea power, and were now hoping to attain as much of a stronghold in the Americas as they had done in the East Indies. The Protestant bigotry of the Dutch Calvinists, however, made them particularly antagonistic towards non-European cultures. Maurits, a true humanist, was fortunately an exceptionally enlightened man who did much to reconcile the Brazilians to Dutch rule, and was strongly opposed both to the economic exploitation of the local peoples and to Calvinist intolerance towards them. A renowned patron of science and the arts, he hoped to instil the values of northern European civilisation into tropical Brazil while also undertaking studies of its natural history and peoples. The scientific and artistic team that he brought with him from Holland included the physician Willem Pies, who was to make a pioneering contribution to tropical medicine, and the cartographer, astronomer and naturalist George Marcgraf, whose *Historia naturalis Brasiliae* would be the most authoritative work on this subject up to the time of Humboldt. To house all the materials that he and his team amassed in the tropics, Maurits commissioned in The Hague one of the major classical structures of seventeenth-century Holland – the Mauritshuis.

Six artists came with Maurits to Brazil, though the principal pictorial duties seem to have been assumed by Post and Eckhout. Post – the brother of the leading Dutch classicist architect, Pieter Post – was the team's main topographical artist, and is generally claimed as the first European landscape painter to have worked in America. He travelled extensively around the country, sometimes with Maurits, and had the particular task of documenting the buildings and fortifications erected by the Dutch during their rule. These structures often appear as incidental features in serene, objectively observed landscapes that have earned Post the ridiculous nickname of the 'Canaletto of Brazil'. More absurdly he has been referred to as a 'seventeenth-century Douanier Rousseau', on the grounds, presumably, that there is something naïve about the incongruous presence of exotic animals and plant-life in landscapes composed in a simple, horizontally-arranged Dutch manner, with large, unbroken expanses of sky and water, and flat countryside seen from a slight elevation. One hundred and twenty of Post's Brazilian views have survived, but of these only six were definitely painted in Brazil. The rest probably date from after his return to Haarlem in 1644, when, with characteristic Dutch common sense, he realised that the best way of surviving in the highly competitive landscape market was to be the sole Dutch specialist in tropical views.

Eckhout was a more remarkable artist than Post, even if he has been described, inexplicably, as the more 'primitif' of the two. Charged partly with the drawing of plants and animals, he produced the studies that were later crudely engraved for Marcgraf's *Historia*. But it was as the official recorder of the local Indian tribes that he displayed his originality and freshness of vision. Whereas an artist of classical, Italianate leanings might have got away with mannered, heroic portrayals of Indians, a Dutch painter who did so would probably have disappointed his compatriots, who by now had become used to a high level of naturalism. Eckhout's drawings of Tapuya and Tupi Indians are evidently drawn from life, and, for the first time in the representation of tribesmen, show their subjects in a startlingly lifelike manner. An even greater achievement, however, was to have maintained such a manner in his finished oil paintings, most notably the extraordinary *Tapuya Dance*, which is not only the earliest painting of native people in a ceremonial act, but also perhaps the first western work of art to capture the movements and postures of such people without resort to classical prototype. Equally innovatory, if also more staged in appearance, are his six ethnic portraits of the early 1640s. The first full-length figure paintings of exotic people in western art, these works were also intended to convey detailed information about the way of life and natural habitat of their subjects. Their combination of artistry and wealth of ethnographic and geographical information would make them model works of art for Alexander Humboldt, whose writings were to be the principal inspiration for travelling artists in America in the nineteenth century.

Yet, unperceived by Humboldt, and a telling indication of the impossibility of the innocent eye, is an underlying moral message behind these apparently straightfor-ward naturalistic works. The portraits of the Tapuyas are deliberately contrasted with those of the Tupis in such a way as to suggest the savagery of those whom the Dutch had failed repeatedly to civilise (the Tapuyas) and the mildness and adaptability to change of the Tupis, who are presented as the ideal people for the imposition of colonial values. The Tupis adequately cover their genitalia, and do not deform their faces with ornaments or indulge in body painting; furthermore they are depicted against a civilised backcloth featuring such symbols of colonial prosperity as riverboats, a plantation, and a manioc root – the staple food of the Dutch colony. In contrast, the tattooed, facially deformed and practically naked Tapuyas are set against a complete wilderness and revealed as cannibals. Eckhout's famous portrait

Frans Post, *Sao Francis River and Fort Maurits, Brazil*; oil on canvas, Musée du Louvre. Though executed in Brazil, the trees and the animal in the foreground are among the few signs that this is not a Dutch landscape.

of a Tapuya woman seems so natural and matter-of-fact that it comes almost as a shock to realise that she is carrying parts of the human body, as well as a club that was used to crush the skulls of prisoners destined for cannibal feasts. The artist leaves us with no room for doubt as to which style of life is to be preferred.

The paintings of Post and Eckhout are isolated phenomena, and it was not until the early nineteenth century that travelling artists would produce comparably memorable images of the American scene. The study and exploration of much of Central and South America remained throughout this period strictly controlled by the Spanish, who put the interior strictly out of bounds to artists and scientists. As for North America, the study of the interior during the colonial period was mainly left to surveyors, a number of whom were third-rate artists often imitating the Claudian-style landscapes of their English contemporaries. Europeans, meanwhile, seem to have been interested less in the North American landscape than in the native Americans, who, from the time of White, were increasingly incorporated as exotic elements in European paintings, sculptures and decorative schemes. Few of the many seventeenth- and eighteenth-century representations of Indians were by artists who had actually lived among them, and of these works hardly any were truly impartial ones, rendered without references to cruelty or to notions of the 'noble savage'. Only later, with the opening up of America's far west, did Indian subject-matter take on a new seriousness, inspired by a curiosity both scientific and sentimental in a people whose existence was increasingly threatened.

The early nineteenth century saw the coming of age of North American art, as technical mastery came to be allied to a recognition of the idiosyncratic qualities of the American environment. Following Alexander Mackenzie's pioneering journey across North America in 1793, the knowledge of this environment began expanding at a prodigious rate, and was accompanied by a more scientific attitude on the part of the artist. To a far greater extent than his romantic European counterpart, the American artist who travelled in search of the exotic found himself venturing into the wilderness like a scientist exploring new terrain. It was no coincidence that one of the greatest American artists of the early years of the century should have been the famous ornithologist and natural history illustrator John James Audubon, whose insistence on drawing birds and other animals in their natural habitat led to his spending thirty-five years engaged in arduous journeys on foot and horseback, and by canoe. Audubon's principal achievement, his four illustrated volumes of *The Birds of America* (1827-38), was described at the time as 'the most magnificent monument that art has ever raised to nature'.

A younger contemporary of Audubon was George Catlin, who devoted himself to the recording of the Indians of the American west with the same mixture of scientific thoroughness and romantic passion with which Audubon had studied American birds. Brought up in rural New York, in a world dominated by hunting and fishing, he acquired an early fascination with Indians that was doubtless fuelled by the tale

Albert Eckhout, *Tapuya War Dance*, c.1641-3; oil on canvas, National Museum of Denmark. A scene illustrating the savagery of the Tapuyas, whom the Dutch had repeatedly failed to tame.

George Catlin, *A Feast*, from *Souvenir of the North American Indians*, vol. 1; pencil, Museum of Mankind, London. Catlin, in his notes to this drawing, describes the scene thus: 'Mah-to-toh-pa (the Four Bears), war-chief of the Mandans, entertaining the author in his wig-wam by feasting him on a "roast rib of Buffalo"'.

George Catlin, *Assiniboin Indian*, from *Souvenir of the North American Indians*, vol. 2; pencil, Museum of Mankind, London. Catlin was deeply concerned for the future of native Americans. The sketch on the right shows 'wi-jun-jon (the pigeon's egg head), son of the head chief, on his way to Washington in a beautiful native costume'; on the left he is shown 'returning from Washington to his native wig-wam, in a colonel's *undress*'.

George Catlin, *The Author Painting a Chief in an Indian Village*, frontispiece to *Letters and Notes on North American Indians*, vol. 1, London, 1841; Beinecke Rare Book and Manuscript Library, New Haven.

of his mother's capture during a massacre in Philadelphia in 1778. Trained in the law, and active initially as a barrister, Catlin was a self-taught artist whose short career as a society portraitist came to a head after executing what a friend of his called 'the worst full-length which the city of New York possesses'. He made perhaps the right decision to go on afterwards to the west, where, in the words of this same friend, 'he has no competitor among the Black Hawks and the White Eagles, and nothing to ruffle his mind in the shape of criticism'. According to Catlin himself, it was a decision reached after the visit to Philadelphia of a group of western Indians on their way to Washington. From that moment onwards, he claimed, he was determined that 'nothing short of the loss of my life shall prevent me visiting their country, and becoming their historian'.

Between 1830 and 1836 Catlin made no less than five trips through the western plains, and produced more than six hundred paintings that would later be exhibited as 'Catlin's Indian Gallery'. In compiling such a collection he saw himself as rescuing for posterity the looks and customs of a 'truly lofty and noble' but ultimately 'doomed' race. Though in his writings he made the inevitable comparisons between the Indians and the ancient Greeks, he did not idealise them in his paintings and portrayed them instead with the objectivity of the true ethnographer.

OVERLEAF LEFT Albert Eckhout, *Tupi Woman and Child*, 1641; oil on canvas, National Museum of Denmark.

OVERLEAF RIGHT Albert Eckhout, *Tapuya Woman*, 1641; oil on canvas, National Museum of Denmark.
These two paintings form a study in contrasts between a tribe which has been successfully colonised by the Dutch (page 118), and one which has not (page 119).

Karl Bodmer, *Interior of a Mandan Earth Lodge Winter Hut*, 1833-34; Joslyn Art Museum, Omaha, Nebraska; Gift of the Enron Art Foundation. Bodmer's detailed and assured rendering of a Mandan dwelling shows up the technical limitations of Catlin's (page 116).

Factual accuracy, he insisted, was more important to him than creating a finished work of art. When he first exhibited the paintings in 1837, he tried to forestall any criticism on artistic grounds by pleading with the viewer to

make due allowance for the unfinished condition in which many of the paintings are exhibited – the author of these works has travelled, for seven years past, under peculiar privations and difficulties in procuring these sketches; and his canvass has been carried the whole way with him, and the greater part of the paintings stand exactly in the same state as they were made in the villages of the different tribes.

Such was his concern to promote accuracy over the purely aesthetic that he often had Indian agents, army officers or other officials signing certificates of authenticity attesting that a particular Indian portrait 'was painted from life . . . and that the Indian sat in the costume in which it is painted'.

The fact that his portraits were so truthful and so undistorted by fanciful or sentimental notions might partly explain why he had so many difficulties in selling his Indian Gallery. After failing to interest an American buyer he went in 1839 to Europe, where the subject-matter of his works was bound to have an even greater exotic appeal than it did in his home country. An exhibition of his collection at London's Egyptian Hall in Piccadilly attracted the likes of Dickens and Queen

Victoria, but he soon had to drum up support for the pictures by devising a sort of Wild West Show in which eventually real members of the Ojibway and Ioway tribes participated. In 1845 he took the show and his still unsold pictures to Paris, where the ethnic exotic has always appealed to intellectuals. One of these was Delacroix, who reacted to Catlin's Indians in the same way as he had done several years previously to the inhabitants of North Africa: he saw in them the ancient world revived. Alexander Humboldt also attended, and recognised the great ethnographic value in the pictures, so much so that, ten years later, he was able to persuade the King of Prussia to buy 104 of the drawings and ten of the oils. However, the only person to have found any artistic merit in Catlin's works was apparently Baudelaire, who went against the commonly held and perhaps justifiable opinion that Catlin was an 'intrepid traveller' but a 'mediocre painter'. In any case the bulk of the pictures were unsold until after Catlin's bankruptcy in later life, when they were acquired by a Philadelphia boilermaker, who stored them in a cellar.

Americans were not the only artists to undertake early journeys to the American west. Hot on Catlin's heels came the Swiss artist Karl Bodmer, who in 1832 embarked on a journey to the prairies as a draughtsman to Prince Maximilian of Wied-Neuwied, who was preparing a sequel to a scientific book of travels in Brazil. After wintering at Robert Owen's utopian New Harmony in Indiana (where the natural history artist Lesueur had been staying in the previous decade), the party emulated Catlin by sailing down the Missouri in the newly inaugurated steamship service run by the American Fur Company. As with most other early travellers to the west, they used as bases the Company's fortified trading posts, which were convenient places to establish initial contact with the Indians.

The expedition that Bodmer accompanied was fired in its scientific principles by the encyclopaedic vision of Humboldt, and it studied Indian life in a much broader context than Catlin had done. Bodmer was also a far more talented artist than Catlin, and was able to combine a fine eye for detail with a powerful sense of composition and atmosphere; the popular potential of his sketches was accentuated in the greatly dramatised prints made after them, such as the one of a bedraggled Indian woman contemplating rotting corpses thrust up on trees against a spectacular cloudscape.

Even without the distortions necessitated by artistic licence and popular appeal, Bodmer's representations of Indians, like those of Catlin, are misleading in that they give an impression of a timeless people living in pure, unspoilt surroundings. Only in one work does Bodmer suggest the vast changes to Indian society that already have been brought about by contact with white men, in particular the fur traders: in this work Prince Maximilian and his party are shown outside Fort Clark exchanging gifts with the Indians, one of whom has already cheerfully and ridiculously placed a top hat over his head-dress.

The fur traders and the trading posts feature often in the works of Alfred Jacob Miller, the artist who in 1839 accompanied the Scottish aristocrat Sir William Drummond Stewart on a tour through the fur districts of the Rocky Mountain West. Miller was only too conscious of the way in which the traders and others were eroding the traditional Indian way of life, but in his works he preferred to portray the

OPPOSITE Karl Bodmer, *Assiniboin Medicine Sign*, 1833; watercolour, Joslyn Art Museum, Omaha, Nebraska; Gift of the Enron Art Foundation. Bodmer was the first artist to capture the haunting strangeness of the West.

Frank Buchser, *Indian Camp at Fort Laramie*, 1866; oil on canvas, Oeffentliche Kunstsammlung Basel, Kunstmuseum. Buchser's *plein air* oil sketches are among the first works to treat Indian subjects essentially as pictorial motifs rather than as objects of romantic or anthropological interest.

Indians as the inhabitants of a simple, idyllic world for which the white man would happily abandon the advantages of civilisation. This world is made all the more Arcadian by the presence of half-naked Indian women who play around un-selfconsciously as if in some Rococo painting, and patiently tend to the trappers' needs and well-being. But, as with all Arcadias, the beauty of the one evoked by Miller is enhanced by its very fragility, by the sense of a Golden Age that can never last. In the commentary to one of his drawings, of a Kansas Indian gazing at a buffalo's head, Miller predicted that 'In a few, very few years, the Indians too will be swept from the face of the world, and the places that now know them, shall behold them no more – forever.' Nostalgia and sentimentality of this kind would characterise the work of the many artists who, from the end of the nineteenth century onwards, would turn to Indian subject-matter in the same way that their contemporaries in Europe turned to vanishing scenes of traditional rural life: as a momentary escape from the realities of the modern, urban world.

Alfred Jacob Miller, *Snake Girl Swinging*; Beinecke Rare Book and Manuscript Library, New Haven. Strong echoes of Fragonard colour this idyllic rendering of Indian life.

The primitive beauty that artists found in the lives of the Indians was also reflected in the magnificently extensive and unspoilt natural surroundings in which these people lived. Yet though Catlin, Bodmer, Miller and others had been quick to exploit the figurative possibilities laid open by the development of the American West, travelling artists were much slower to respond to the challenge of depicting the newly discovered landscapes – landscapes of a scale and grandeur that few artists would have experienced elsewhere. The earliest outstanding landscape paintings of the West date from after the mid-nineteenth century, at a time when the railroad was beginning to have a devastating effect on the environment.

The Europeans continued to maintain their general lack of interest in the American landscape, though it was another Swiss traveller, the Basle-born Frank Buchser, who was one of the first great artists to capture the special appeal of the landscapes of western Kansas and Colorado. Buchser, a radical who had fought under Garibaldi in 1849, was one of the most itinerant of the nineteenth-century artist travellers, and he had already journeyed extensively around southern Spain and Morocco before coming to America in 1865. In the late summer of 1866 he embarked on his journey west, travelling by train all the way to Fort Laramie, an experience that evidently exhilarated him while also making him aware of the destructive capacity of the railroad. The delicate and evocative oil sketches that resulted from this trip evinced the following reaction from the Baltimore *Catholic Mirror*:

How little idea have most of us of the magnificence and beauty of our land! We read in the dailies of the Plains, Forts Kearney, Laramie, &c., . . . and we associate them with such drearly dismal scenes; yet with what a charm to the eye of a foreigner have these glimpses of true nature. A spirit of enterprise too will soon work changes. 'There is to be a railroad there', says the artist by our side, recalling us from our reverie, 'and that will spoil all.'

Buchser's intimate and painterly western landscapes would influence a number of younger artists who came out here. But it was a very different and quintessentially American style of landscape painting – a style which stands in relation to Buchser's art as Hollywood does to the European art movie – that would render more successfully the sublimity of the American West. Patriotic, ambitious, exclamatory, symbolic, mystical in its grand design, and yet scientific in the accuracy of its detailing, this was a style that has its origins in the art and writings of Thomas Cole, founder of the Hudson River School. Though heavily steeped in the art of such European masters as Claude, Salvator Rosa, John Martin and Turner, Cole dedicated much of his art to what he considered a moral quest to reveal the beauty of American nature, which for him was distinguished by a wildness lacking in civilised Europe, where 'the primitive features of scenery have long since been destroyed or modified'. Most of his ideas were contained in his influential 'Essay on American Scenery' (1834), in which he wrote that in America 'all nature is new to Art', and that the American wilderness was a vestige of Paradise.

A later associate of the Hudson River School, and also one of the first of these artists to paint in the West, was Albert Bierstadt. After training in the Düsseldorf Academy of Art, he returned to his home town of New Bedford, Massachusetts, from where, in April 1859, he set off on the first of three western journeys that would establish his reputation as the foremost competitor of Frederic Church in the field of monumental New World landscapes. Declaring at the outset of this first journey that he would be 'making sketches of the scenery, and studying the manners and customs of the Indians, preparatory to painting a series of large pictures', he spent seven months in the present states of Kansas, Nebraska, Wyoming and Colorado. For much of the time he travelled with a government survey expedition led by Colonel Frederick W. Lander, a notable patriot and proponent of the visual arts who believed that artists would reach their highest peaks of excellence were they to direct their art to the 'patriotic sentiments of the people'. The fact that Bierstadt, in accompanying Lander, was travelling through parts of America that had never before been visited by the artist gave a patriotic element to his whole venture, and contributed to the success of the main canvas that would result from this trip.

OVERLEAF Albert Bierstadt, *The Rocky Mountains, Lander's Peak*, 1863; oil on canvas, The Metropolitan Museum of Art, Rogers Fund, 1907. A composite, blockbuster of a canvas which brings together the main impressions of Bierstadt's first encounter with the American West, when travelling with the government surveyor, Colonel Lander, in 1859.

This work – the first of Bierstadt's epic canvases of the West – seems to have been first planned at a time in the trip when he and an artist companion had briefly separated from Lander's party, and were living precariously on bread and water, not daring to fire a gun for fear of revealing their whereabouts to 'hostile Indians, tribes of whom had murdered three white travellers'. With the help of photographs, oil sketches, and even Indian and other artefacts that he had assembled on his journey, Bierstadt concentrated for many months on his return to New Bedford on a large painting of the Rocky Mountains, based on a view from near the headwaters of the Rio Colorado, and with a central peak named in homage to Lander. A leaflet accompanying the exhibited painting emphatically stressed the work's topographical accuracy, which Bierstadt was as keen on proving as he was the work's anthropological truthfulness. When first shown in New York, the work was surrounded by some of the artefacts that had been used to recreate the Indian encampment in the foreground; and later, when on display at the Metropolitan Fair of the United States Sanitary Commission, Bierstadt even went as far as to make a life-sized reconstruction of this encampment peopled with real Indians.

American art critics, who often seemed to value topographical verisimilitude and scientific accuracy in a landscape painter more than they did artistic vision, were not wholly convinced by Bierstadt's claims for *The Rocky Mountains, Lander's Peak*. And they would find ever more cause for complaint in the course of Bierstadt's subsequent career, when his imagination grew in keeping with the ever expanding size of his canvases. His second journey to the West, in 1863, would produce perhaps the most ambitious and memorable paintings of his career. On this occasion he travelled with Fitz Hugh Ludlow, a writer and hashish eater who would describe the journey in *The Heart of the Continent*. Ludlow's book alternates passages of dreary factual objectivity with others written in a heightened state that recalls the euphoria and exaggerated responses of Humboldt's accounts of travelling through South America. An ecstatic highpoint of the journey was apparently reached after the two men had moved on from the Rockies and reached California's Yosemite Valley, which they entered with the expectation of 'going to the original site of the Garden of Eden'. The whole valley seemed to them like 'the tenth foundation-stone of John's apocalyptic heaven . . . Far to the westward, widening more and more, it opens into the bosom of great mountain-ranges, – into a field of perfect light, misty by its own excess, – into an unspeakable suffusion of glory created from the phoenix-pile of the dying sun.'

The spirit of Ludlow's description of Yosemite was perfectly captured in what was not only one of Bierstadt's largest canvases but also one of his most sublime – *The Domes of the Yosemite* (1867). Yet, even when confronted with such exhilarating magnificence, Bierstadt's critics maintained more than ever their petty criterion of accuracy. One such critic was Mark Twain, who, while admiring the detailing of the pines, the boulders and the snow peaks, was most disapproving of the overall atmosphere, and could not help thinking that 'this man has imported this atmosphere from some foreign country, because nothing like it was ever seen in California . . . It is more the atmosphere of Kingdom-Come than of California.' 'As a picture', Twain concluded, 'this work must please, but as a portrait I do not think it will answer. Portraits should be accurate. We do not want this glorified atmosphere smuggled into a part of the Yosemite, where it surely does not belong. I may be wrong, but I still believe that this atmosphere of Mr. Bierstadt's is altogether too gorgeous.'

In transcending science and topography through a sense of the divine in nature, Bierstadt was expressing the ultimate concern of the travelling artist, who has so often been driven on by a vision of a terrestrial Garden of Eden. But the image of Paradise is one which accords less well with the monumental expanses of the American West than with the tropical grandeur of Latin America. It was to the South rather than to the West that Bierstadt's great mentor Frederick Church was drawn, and it was there that Church brought to an exciting climax one of the most adventurous and artistically rewarding phases in the history of artist travellers to exotic lands.

The image of a tropical paradise, the persistent myth of El Dorado, and the 'stimulus of an unexplored country', as George Catlin would later put it, were among the reasons that made Central and South America so enticing to the artist adventurer from the beginning of the nineteenth century onwards. The person who did most to direct the scientific and artistic imagination to these lands was Alexander Humboldt, who in 1799 persuaded the Spanish king Charles IV to issue a passport allowing him and his botanist companion Aimé Bonpland to explore the Latin American interior: the king had apparently been won over by the Prussian's knowledge of Spanish, and by the possibility that Humboldt's training as a mining geologist would lead to the discovery of minerals in the South. The French scientist La Condamine had undertaken a limited expedition to the interior in 1735; but the scientific – and indeed pictorial – knowledge of Spain's American possessions was still limited principally to studies of the coastal districts carried out in the course of such Pacific voyages as those of Cook and Malaspina (whose artists, for instance, were responsible for some of the earliest representations of Tierra del Fuego and Buenos Aires respectively).

Humboldt may not have discovered El Dorado, as Charles IV had hoped, but he found a continent that for him was far richer and more fantastical than that evoked by any of the myths. 'What a fabulous and extravagant country we're in!', he wrote after landing in Venezuela,

Fantastic plants, electric eels, armadillos, monkeys, parrots: and many, many real, half-savage Indians . . . Up till now we've been running around like a couple of mad things; for the first three days we couldn't settle to anything; we'd find one thing, only to abandon it for the next. Bonpland keeps telling me he'll go out of his mind if the wonders don't cease soon.

Apart from accomplishing such explorational feats as sailing into an unknown region of the upper Orinoco and making the first ascent of what was then considered the world's highest mountain (the Ecuadorian peak of Chimborazo), Humboldt's expedition would collect enough scientific data to lay the foundations for modern physical geography and to establish the concept of plant geography. For almost thirty years after his return to Europe in 1804 Humboldt would devote himself to

OVERLEAF Albert Bierstadt, *The Domes of the Yosemite*, 1867; oil on canvas, St Johnsbury Athenæum, Vermont. Bierstadt, in this major work resulting from his second trip out West in 1863, eschews strict naturalism in a painting which unites geology, metaphysics and national celebration.

writing up his South American finds and experiences. Not content with the dry presentation of new information, he attempted even in his most theoretical works to instil in the reader a sense of the wonder and excitement that he himself had felt in the tropical world. In his *Aspects of Nature* (1808), which foreshadows many of the ideas contained in his culminating *Cosmos*, he outlined the general character of each of the distinct climactic zones into which he saw the world divided, and emphasised that for him nature in her noblest form was only to be found in the tropics, where in mountainous zones the traveller could observe the whole spectrum of vegetal life as well as study the stars of the northern and southern hemispheres: the nearer the Equator, in his view, the greater the earth's vitality and fecundity.

Humboldt had enormous visual imagination, and believed that images could convey far more effectively than words the impact of Nature in such extreme manifestations as in the tropics. A realisation of the importance of the landscape painter in disseminating a knowledge of distant lands had come to him long before embarking for South America. He had had the revelation after seeing in 1790 some Indian paintings by William Hodges in the London home of Warren Hastings; in *Cosmos* he claimed that these paintings were one of the three main factors in awakening his 'inextinguishable longing to visit the tropics'. In a way that parallels Hodges' plea for an open-minded response to exotic, non-European environments, Humboldt challenged his contemporaries' very limited and Eurocentric view of landscape painting, and urged artists to go off and depict characteristic landscapes from all the different climactic zones, and in particular the tropical one, where vegetation was at its most varied and majestic. 'It would be an enterprise worthy of a great artist', he stressed, 'to study the aspect and character of all these vegetable groups, not merely in hot houses or in the descriptions of botanists but in their native grandeur in the tropical zone'. Championing an expressive role for the landscape artist, Humboldt believed that the northern imagination would be immensely enriched by works that went beyond scientific topography and conveyed 'the living image of that more vigorous nature which other climes display'.

Humboldt himself did not take an artist with him on his travels, but made sketches that the French painter Pierre-Antoine Marchais would use for his illustrations to Humboldt's writings. However, professional artists would play a critical part in popularising the tropics in the wake of Humboldt, when the restrictions preventing foreign explorers in the South American interior began to be lifted. The Viennese artist Thomas Ender accompanied the group of scientists that sailed to Brazil in 1817 on the frigate carrying the Archduchess Leopoldina of Austria to her future husband, Don Pedro, Crown Prince of Brazil: Ender would produce over seven hundred delicate drawings and watercolours of the Brazilian interior in between Bahia and São Paolo. On this same ship, the *Austria*, came two Bavarian scientists – the zoologist Johann Baptist von Spix and the botanist Carl Friedrich Philipp von Martius – who took leave of the Austrians at Rio, and subsequently did for the Amazon what Humboldt had done for the Orinoco: among the magnificent illustrations featured in Martius's *Flora brasiliensis* (1840-46) is one of Martius sketching a tree of such fantastical size as to substantiate the awe-struck travellers' reaction that 'there is more to be found in forests than in books'.

Fourteen years after the *Austria* had set sail for Rio, the young and timorous Charles Darwin joined as scientist an expedition that had as one of its main purposes the charting of the South American coast. Sharing a cabin with him on the *Beagle* was Augustus Earle, who, with his previous knowledge of South America, and extensive experience of travelling in the South Pacific, seemed the perfect artist to be assigned to the expedition. Earle proved as always diverting, sociable and eccentric company; but unfortunately he was already suffering from the ill health that would lead him, eight years later, to die a lonely death in London from 'asthma and debilitation'. Darwin, who took an almost obsessive interest in Earle's health, noted down the artist's every symptom, but was obliged to leave him on board ship during most of the excursions he made after landing at the Brazilian coast. The ailing and very popular Earle had eventually and reluctantly to be left at Montevideo, where he was replaced by another English artist, Conrad Martens.

The *Beagle*'s captain Robert FitzRoy took an immediate liking to Earle's replace-

Conrad Martens, *Valparaiso*, *c.*1832; pencil, British Museum. In addition to the bold, atmospheric studies executed whilst travelling with Darwin on the *Beagle*, Martens completed numerous delicate and more conventional sketches such as this one.

ment, and, in his characteristically boisterous style, described him as 'a *stone pounding artist* – who exclaims in his sleep "*think of me*" standing upon a pinnacle of the Andes – or sketching a foreign glacier!!!' Darwin, who formed a close friendship with Martens, found him 'very unlike to Earle's eccentric character' and probably fired him with his enthusiasm for Humboldt, whose writings he had taken with him on the voyage. The many watercolours and drawings that Martens did on the journey – either from the boat or on such inland trips as the one up the Santa Cruz river in Patagonia – would in any case have met with Humboldt's approval through combining accurate observation with a powerful sense of atmosphere, which would have been quite beyond Earle's technical capacities.

For artists the exploration of the Latin American interior did more than just open up an exciting new world of natural curiosities: it also brought them into contact with ancient civilisations no less fascinating or important than that of Egypt. Humboldt, through the inclusion of some archaeological illustrations in his *Views of the Mountains and Monuments of the Native Peoples of America* (Paris, 1810) had been effectively the first to introduce Europe to Aztec carvings and buildings. Shortly afterwards a number of illustrated publications devoted to Aztec and Mayan antiquities appeared, including the *Voyage pittoresque et archéologique dans la partie la plus intéressante du Mexique* (1839) by Jean Frédéric Maximilien de Waldeck, an eccentric aristocrat who portrayed himself being carried by chair on an Indian's back over the Chiapas from Palenque to Ocotzinco. 'The Orient today holds virtually no more secrets for Europe', wrote Waldeck in the expectation that the ancient mysteries of the Latin American jungle would soon lure away the many Europeans who flocked to North Africa and the Near East.

Living up to this prediction, the English-born artist Frederick Catherwood, having made a name for himself for his sketches of monuments in Egypt and Palestine (see page 50), visited the Yucatan in 1839 in the company of the writer John Lloyd Stephens. Whereas Waldeck's illustrations of Mayan monuments are in the eighteenth-century tradition of objective draughtsmanship, Catherwood's are deeply romantic and atmospheric, with the ruined buildings and carvings exuding a sinister, mysterious power in the middle of dark and sometimes moonlit jungles filled with snakes, leopards, and other hidden dangers. These illustrations captured the imagination of the distinguished historian of America's ancient civilisations, William Prescott, and also helped to establish the popular vision of the lost world of the Mayas.

Catherwood belongs to the greatest generation of travelling artists to have painted the Latin American interior – a generation which travelled independent of any scientific mission, and with motives that were primarily pictorial and romantic rather than academic. These were the true artistic inheritors of Humboldt, and indeed several of them had had direct encouragement from him. As an old man Humboldt would be able to say that what Hodges had achieved in the South Seas had been done in tropical America 'in a much grander style and with greater mastery' by Johann Moritz Rugendas and Ferdinand Bellerman – a reference to two German artists who had been among the earliest landscapists to convey the qualities of the Latin American environment evoked in Humboldt's writings.

Rugendas first came to Latin America in 1821, as a nineteen-year-old draughtsman on an expedition that the Russian Consul-General, Baron von Langsdorff, planned to lead to the Brazilian interior. He ended up staying for four years, producing on his own account a large body of drawings that he managed to have published after showing them to Humboldt on his return to Europe. Encouraged again by Humboldt, he returned to Latin America in 1831 and spent the next sixteen years wandering around Mexico, Chile, Peru, Bolivia, Argentina, Uruguay and Brazil. His restlessness is conveyed in bold, impressionistic sketches that are radiant with all the continent's colour, life and light. Bellerman, in contrast, was a much more meticulous artist whose drawings and watercolours – executed while travelling

Martin Heade, *Cattleya Orchid and Three Brazilian Hummingbirds*, 1871; oil on wood, National Gallery of Art, Washington; Gift of The Morris and Gwendolyn Cafritz Foundation. Obsessed with both orchids and hummingbirds, Heade devised a genre of painting which falls between landscape and still life.

Frederick Catherwood, *The Mouth of the Wells of Itza*, 1843; ink and wash over pencil, The Brooklyn Museum. An excellent example of the way in which Catherwood made detailed archaeological draughtsmanship come alive.

around Venezuela in the 1840s on a grant which Humboldt obtained for him from the Prussian king – render the claustrophobia, terror, mystery and untouched grandeur of the landscapes.

In citing as exemplars of landscape art the Latin American works of Rugendas, Bellerman, and other, lesser German artists, Humboldt, in his *Personal Narrative of Travels to the Equinoctial Regions of America* (1852-3), might have piqued the nationalistic pride of the many North American artists who, from the late 1830s until the 1870s, headed south to create what has recently been described as a 'tropical Renaissance'. Humboldt's writings were certainly an important influence behind this North American influx, but there were other factors involved, even perhaps a fascination with the idea of a greater America stretching from Newfoundland to Tierra del Fuego. Escapism too played an important part – and not just escapism of the romantic kind that would later lead Gauguin to the South Seas. A number of artists escaped to Latin America for the same practical reasons that made the western gangster Butch Cassidy do so in 1902: to be in a place that was generally perceived as being beyond the law, or, at least, beyond extradition treaties and debt collectors. The photographer Eadweard Muybridge secretly departed to Central America to avoid arrest and imprisonment for murdering his wife's lover and allegedly poisoning his wife.

More commonly, artists went south when faced with mounting financial difficulties. One such artist was Francis Drexel, who fled his native Switzerland to avoid conscription, and settled in Philadelphia, where he worked as a drawing instructor and portraitist before losing both his job and all his commissions as a result of slanderous attacks made against him; an unsuccessful libel suit proved the final straw and forced him to try and make a living in South America from selling prints and paintings of Simon Bolivar. In the case of George Catlin, who spent a total of five years in Latin America in the 1850s, the decision to come here was connected as much with financial considerations as with genuine curiosity. His interest in these lands might originally have been stimulated by his dealings with Humboldt, through whom he probably secured his introduction to Bonpland in Uruguay. But the debts that he had accrued in Europe from his Indian Gallery had been so great that he would have been put in prison had he stayed there. What is more, Catlin was one of several artists who took the El Dorado myth very seriously: dreams of discovering fabled treasures had already been formed before leaving Europe, and drew him immediately on arrival in South America to the Crystal Mountains in Brazil, where he spent considerably less time sketching than hunting for gold.

More openly artistic motives were behind the Latin American journeys of the three most interesting North American artists to have worked here – Frederic Church and his two friends Martin Johnson Heade and Louis Mignot. Heade, a peripatetic artist, was the most single-minded of the three in his vision of the tropics: in his travels in the 1860s around Brazil, Nicaragua, Colombia and Panama, he concentrated his attentions largely on the humming-bird, which he portrayed in close-up against a background of exotic flowers. Heade himself denied for these works 'the importance of a scientific character', and saw in the humming-bird – and in particular its ability to spring to vibrant life with the first rays of the sun – his

PREVIOUS PAGES Frederic Church, *The Heart of the Andes*, 1859; oil on canvas, The Metropolitan Museum of Art; Bequest of Margaret E. Dows, 1909. A large oil sketch for this canvas showed entirely different foreground vegetation; the snow-capped peak is Chimborazo.

OPPOSITE After Frederick Catherwood, *Colossal Head at Izmal*, lithograph by Henry Warren from Catherwood's *Views of Ancient Monuments in Central America, Chiapas and Yucatan*, London 1844. Works such as these, so heavy in atmosphere and a sense of adventure, might well have influenced childhood and Hollywood conceptions of the Central American jungle.

personal symbol of the vitality and exuberance of the tropical world. Mignot was similarly unscientific in his attitude towards art, and in this differed greatly from Church, whom he accompanied on the latter's trip to Ecuador in 1857. Church, whose works were often used for geographical demonstrations, was interested, like his mentor Humboldt, primarily in the drama and sublimity of Ecuador's Andean scenery. Mignot, meanwhile, was more like a tropical Guardi, and preferred to evoke mistily the stagnant and haunting stillness of the swamps and rivers of the Ecuadorean lowlands.

Mignot, for whom the Equador trip was merely one episode in a life of wandering, was a romantic in that he was someone who travelled out of an innate restlessness, and projected his own self onto the landscapes he saw. Church, in contrast, though the author of some of the works that best fulfil the romantic concept of the Sublime, was a more methodical and structured traveller, who treated his trips like scientifically informed reconnaissances, carried them out with an almost military precision, and always returned to a stable home base from where he would turn his innumerable sketches from nature into finished canvases.

An enormous enthusiasm for Humboldt's writings was a central factor in Church's desire to go to Latin America, and also helped to determine the parts of the continent that he was particularly interested in. The first of his two trips there was carried out in 1853 with Cyrus Field, the future successful projector of the transatlantic cable. Beginning their journey at the mouth of the Magdalena river in Colombia, they sailed along that river for six hundred miles before continuing on mule-back for a further four months; after 'trailing along with eight or nine mules in Indian file zig-zagging up the Andes to Quito', they passed the Equator and Chimborazo, and finally reached the Pacific at the Ecuadorean port of Guayaquil, from where they returned to the United States by way of Panama. As well as assembling numerous sketchbooks and individual sketches in pencil, watercolour, gouache and oil, Church had also been able to indulge his and Field's entrepreneurial instincts by visiting a number of gold, silver and emerald mines along the route.

Church's second journey, with Louis Mignon, was a much simpler and shorter affair, and comprised two months in Ecuador concentrating on what had been the two literal and metaphorical highpoints of his previous trip – the mountains of Chimborazo and Cotopaxi, later the subjects of three of the most popular and sensational works of his career. Cotopaxi, one of the world's most spectacular volcanoes, was particularly impressive on this second trip, as it was now in a state of continuous eruption, and belching immense clouds of smoke and debris.

Church's reputation as a painter of monumental and dramatic landscapes had been clinched by a huge canvas of *Niagara* which had been exhibited three months before his Ecuador trip. Thousands of visitors had gone to see the painting, which differed from the countless earlier representations of the celebrated falls by its attenuated horizontal proportions, the symbolical power invested by a rainbow, and by its placing of the spectator's vantage-point at the very edge of the great drop of water: for the nineteenth-century viewer the impact of such a work must have been wholly cinematic.

With all the material that Church had acquired on his two Latin American journeys, he clearly hoped for a repeat of *Niagara*'s success. It was not until after his return from Ecuador in 1857 that he was finally able to bring to completion a painting conceived on his first Latin American trip and based on a combination of sketches, memories and his mind's eye. Featuring the white profile of Chimborazo rising up above an idyllic tropical river scene, this work, *The Heart of the Andes* (1859), brought together the microcosmic range of natural elements that Humboldt had so admired in Ecuador: in the words of one of those who wrote about it at the time, it

PREVIOUS PAGES Frederic Church, *Cotopaxi*,
1862; oil on canvas, The Detroit Institute of
Arts. A study of nature in turmoil to
counterbalance the idyllic view of the
tropics portrayed in *The Heart of the Andes*
(pages 138-9).

was 'the complete condensation of South America'. The critical and popular impact
of this work proved to be even greater than that of *Niagara*, and drew more paying
crowds than any other painting in the history of nineteenth-century American art.
On the closing day of the New York single-picture exhibition in which it was first
shown, the future Impressionist painter John Ferguson Weir was 'told by the
doorkeeper that the paying attendance for that day was more than six thousand
visitors'.

After enjoying a similar success in London, Church's European agent hoped to
take the painting to Berlin, principally, in the words of Church, so as 'to have the
satisfaction of placing before Humboldt a transcript of the scenery which delighted
his eyes sixty years ago and which he has pronounced to be the finest in the world'.
However, unknown to Church when he wrote these words, Humboldt had died
three days previously, thus missing out on the opportunity to have seen the first
major painting to have fulfilled his ideal vision of the tropical landscape.

Church's claim to be 'considered as the artistic Humboldt of the New World' was
finally vindicated, according to his contemporaries, with his second major Andean
work, *Chimborazo* (1862). This painting was probably intended as a response to
Darwin's *On the Origin of Species*, which had been published in the year that *The Heart
of the Andes* had been completed, and had been dismissed by Church's naturalist
friend Louis Agassiz as 'poor, very poor'. While Agassiz set out to disprove Darwin's
theories by planning an expedition to the heart of Brazil, Church attempted in
Chimborazo to portray a volcanic landscape which seemed to contain the secrets of
the earth's origins. Church had been fascinated by Humboldt's description of a
volcano that was not only the 'most beautiful and regular of the colossal summits of
the high Andes' but also 'the most dreadful . . . of the kingdom of Quito'. After his
first trip to Ecuador he had painted the mountain in a way that emphasised its
geometric beauty and serene surroundings; but, after seeing the mountain in a new,
violent light in 1857, he chose to depict all its latent powers of destruction. His
Cotopaxi of 1862 is a turbulent riposte to *The Heart of the Andes*, and substitutes the
latter's vision of the tropics as a Garden of Eden with a sublime cataclysmic vision
suggestive of how the world was originally created by God.

In a pamphlet intended for the inaugural exhibition of the work in New York,
Church's friend and travelling companion on a 1859 trip to Labrador and Newfoundland, the Reverend Louis Noble, imaginatively evoked the geographical
setting that had inspired Church:

Earthquakes convulse, lavas overwhelm, waters wash and excavate, gather in . . . the
hollows & abysses, rush through fissures & over precipices, clouds & electricity storms the
summits, tropical sunshine touches all with warmth and brightness. Hence that marvelous
mingling of the Seasons – Spring, Summer & Autumn, below & all around – above, the
arctic snows.

Before embarking on a work summarising his experiences with Noble searching for
icebergs, Church produced the third and last of his Andean blockbusters, *Chimborazo*
(1864). Returning to the same motif and mood of *The Heart of the Andes*, he created
once again a bold juxtaposition between the throbbing vitality of the jungle lowland

and the calm, imposing whiteness of Chimborazo, which is here suspended in space like some ethereal apparition. 'But where is Chimborazo?', asked an English critic, 'Oh, it is far above, islanded in the soft blue of the upper heavens, above an expanse of this sky-like vapour, like a dome of tender sunny cloud, a thing entirely pertaining to heaven, and having nothing whatever to do with earth, but to present it with an image of heavenly peace, an object to inspire heavenly fancies and yearnings.'

There is an almost Japanese quality in Church's final rendering of Chimborazo – a quality that would also be present, but to a much greater extent, in the pictures painted three years later by the last of the great nineteenth-century artists to have worked in Latin America: James Whistler. Though Whistler is not generally thought of as a 'travelling artist', he was a wandering expatriate whose restlessness took him in 1866 on a ten month tour along the South American coast. It was at the Chilean port of Valparaiso that he executed a series of delicately suggestive canvases representing his first successful attempt to order his compositions according to the principles of oriental design.

Church and Whistler could hardly be more different artists, but with the Hokusai-like Chimborazo of the one, and the oriental-style compositions of the other, there is further evidence that at the back of so many visions of distant lands is a vision of the Orient.

ABOVE AND OVERLEAF Frederic Church, Chimborazo, 1864; oil on canvas, The Henry E. Huntington Library and Art Gallery, California. Humboldt's beloved peak is seen here rising above the river Guayaquil.

OVERLEAF, RIGHT James Abbott McNeill Whistler, *The Morning after the Revolution, Valparaiso*, 1866; oil on canvas, Hunterian Art Gallery, University of Glasgow, Birnie Philip Gift. Whistler was based in Valparaiso between March and September 1866 and witnessed there the bombardment of the harbour by the Spanish fleet – an incident which probably gave rise to this painting's enigmatic title.

6

The Heart of Africa and the Polar Regions

By the middle of the nineteenth century the last places in the world that continued to pose major challenges to the explorer were the African interior south of the Sudan, and the polar regions. The story of the journeys to uncover the source of the Nile, to determine the existence of arctic passages to Asia, and to conquer the North and South Poles, is one that involved quite exceptional hardships and dangers, and would result in some of the most popular accounts in the history of nineteenth- and twentieth-century travel literature. However, it is a story that cannot be supplemented with any great wealth of artistic material.

The African interior, which had been rumoured since the time of Herodotus to be one vast desert, only began to be an important focus of explorational and colonial ambitions from the late eighteenth century onwards. Britain, after losing her economic footing in America in 1783, turned optimistically to Africa, a continent of limitless potential. The African Association – the precursor of the Royal Geographical Society – was founded in 1788, and started sending investigators such as Mungo Park to areas that were still empty spaces on the map. Between 1800 and 1894 an estimated 394 explorers lost their lives in Africa – a figure only superseded by that of arctic losses.

The most successful of these explorers was David Livingstone, who crossed the continent from coast to coast, disproved once and for all Herodotus's theory of the African interior, and dreamed of a Christian Africa at the crossroads of the world trade routes. In 1858, when his fame had been secured with his *Missionary Travels and Researches*, he proposed to the British government that England and Portugal should continue 'to open South Central Africa to the commerce of the world'. The government responded by putting him in charge of a research mission to the Zambezi river. Livingstone, a loner like so many other of the great African explorers, would have preferred to have been sent alone, but was now compelled to ask for 'a general assistant and "moral agent", an economic botanist, a practical geologist, an engineer, a navigatory officer, and an artist who might also serve as a trader and storekeeper'. The artist chosen was Thomas Baines – one of the very few known European artists to have worked in the African interior in the nineteenth century. The others include Samuel Daniell, a relative of Thomas and William Daniell, who in 1801-2 accompanied Sir John Barrow on a journey to 'the remotest point in the interior of Southern Africa to which Europeans have hitherto penetrated'; another was the German landscape painter Johan Martin Bernatz, who went on a British expedition to Ethiopia in 1841-3, and painted there what was probably the first representation of a mirage.

Samuel Daniell *Hottentot Woman*, *c*.1801-2; the British Library. This was presumably executed when Daniell accompanied Sir John Barrow on his pioneering trip into the South African interior.

Baines was a self-taught painter who would later be remembered as an 'explorer and artist'. Born in King's Lynn, England, in 1820, and later working there as an 'ornamental painter', he settled while still an adolescent in the Cape Colony, where, like Samuel Daniell, he struggled to support himself through his art: 'we need hardly say', wrote one of his contemporaries, 'that for any man to earn a competent living by art in the Cape Colony is always an uphill task'. Distinguishing himself more through his bravery than his artistry, he sketched scenes from the Kaffir Wars of 1848-51 before achieving a reputation as a 'scientific geographer' after travelling in the 1850s in northern Australia. His Australian work led to his being recommended to Livingstone by the Royal Geographical Society; and on his return from the Zambezi, the Society allowed Baines to use a spare room in its headquarters as a studio.

Baines did not get on well with Livingstone, owing to differences arising from his having had to accept 'the somewhat inferior office of storekeeper'. But, after separating briefly from the expedition, he became the first artist to depict the spectacular Victoria Falls, the discovery of which in 1855 had been the most exciting moment of Livingstone's career as an explorer. Perched sometimes on a ledge, tormented by flies, and deafened by the fall of the water, Baines made numerous sketches that were published as lithographs in *The Victoria Falls, Zambezi River, Sketched on the Spot, During the Journey of J. Chapman and T. Baines* (1865). 'In presenting to the public the accompanying views of these magnificent falls', Baines wrote in the preface to this book,

I presume not to compete with the works of those who have so beautifully illustrated more accessible countries. In the interior of Africa, an artist must leave behind him every convenience, and becoming in turn smith, carpenter, tailor, and shoemaker, bullock-driver and astronomical observer, must obtain his sketches and finish his pictures as he can, trusting that any want of artistic finish may be compensated by the faithfulness inseparate from working as much as possible in the actual presence of nature.

Baines, in other words, was an indifferent artist whose works were criticised by his contemporaries for 'his want of finish, and too great glare in their colouring'. 'As an artist', one of his critics concluded, 'Baines' works are very numerous, executed, as too many of them were, very hastily, and almost to supply his daily and pressing wants.'

The recording of arctic and antarctic lands has a much longer if scarcely more distinguished pedigree than that of Equatorial Africa. Much of the history of polar exploration is connected with the search for alternative routes between Europe and Asia, most notably in the unknown seas that washed the northern coasts of Asia and America (respectively the North-East and North-West Passages), and in the mysterious expanse surrounding the North Pole. Among the earliest known drawings by a travelling artist are those attributed to John White showing Newfoundland Eskimos observed during Martin Frobisher's search for a North-West Passage in 1577. John Webber, in the course of Cook's search for a northern passage between the Pacific and Atlantic oceans in 1776, depicted a group of Cook's men firing at seahorses in icy waters; Hodges, meanwhile, when travelling with Cook three years earlier, was perhaps the first artist to convey the special beauty of icebergs – a beauty rendered in words by one of the expedition's accompanying naturalists, Anders Sparrman: 'the glow of the setting sun fell upon this iceberg, which was as clear as crystal, so that its many thousand crevices and chasms shone like gold, in a clear scintillating yellow, while the rest of the mass reflected a rich purple colour'.

The eerie, other-worldly beauty of vast expanses of snow and ice has often been praised by polar explorers, and has often seemed a compensation for putting up with ardours so great that, in the words of Robert Scott's companion Apsley Cherry-Garrard, travellers have begun 'to think of death as a friend'. Sadly, however, virtually all those with artistic responsibilities on the major polar voyages have been amateurs without the technical ability to evoke this beauty with complete success.

The great age of polar travel was initiated in the nineteenth century, when explorers began wintering in polar regions, and making land journeys across them. The original visual records of these trips were largely supplied by naval officers, including Lieutenant Beechey, who in 1818-9 accompanied Edward Parry in what was the first attempt to reach the North Pole by land; his sketches were later engraved by William Westall. John Franklin's polar journeys of 1823 and 1828 were

William Hodges, *The Resolution and Adventure among Icebergs*, 1773; wash, Mitchell Library, State Library of New South Wales. Executed whilst Captain Cook's ships slowly made their way through the Antarctic, this shows that Hodges was no less adept at rendering atmosphere in his drawings than in his paintings.

illustrated by Lieutenant Back, a very able draughtsman as well as an explorer renowned for the unfortunately named 'Back Passage'. Elisha Kent Kane, a Philadelphia doctor who tried in 1853-5 to sail to the North Pole, was a less talented artist than Back, but was lucky enough to have his sketches engraved by the leading American marine painter, James Hamilton: Hamilton's illustrations succeed at times in evoking the character of what Kane described as 'a landscape such as Milton or Dante might imagine, inorganic, desolate, mysterious'. The most prolific of the draughtsmen to have worked in polar regions was the Austrian cartographer Julius Payer, who was another of those who believed that the North Pole was surrounded by open sea. His many sketches of the journey he made in 1874 to try to prove this theory include one in oils of the icy funeral of his ship's chief engineer, Krisch, who had died from pulmonary tuberculosis.

The main objectives of polar travel were not finally achieved until the last years of the nineteenth century and the first years of the twentieth. Though cameras were by this time the standard tool of most travellers, they were still unable to cope with the sub-zero conditions of the polar regions. One of the last instances of art's usefulness as a documentary record of travel must be the crude charcoal and chalk drawings made by Dr Edward Wilson on Robert Scott's Antarctic expedition of 1901-4 and again on the latter's ill-fated march to the South Pole in 1911-12.

But it is to the golden age in the history of the artist traveller – the mid-nineteenth century – that one must return to find one of the sole paintings in which artistry and detailed research come together to capture the beauty and destructiveness of ice-bound seas. Frederic Church, having conquered the tropics, set his sights on the icy north, and in 1859 set off for Newfoundland and Labrador on a voyage that was to be

described in the Reverend Louis L. Noble's *After Icebergs with a Painter* (1861). '"After icebergs!", exclaims a prudent, but imaginary person, as I pencil the title on the front leaf of my note-book.' After deer, after buffalo, after ostriches, all seem acceptable propositions to Noble's imagined sceptic. '"But after icebergs is certainly a cool, if not a novel and perilous adventure. A few climb to the ices of the Andes; but after the ices of Greenland, except by leave of government or your merchant prince, is entirely another thing."'

Noble's book, in which Church is given a heroic, metaphorical status by being referred to constantly as 'the Painter', portrays the artist as an indomitable spirit setting up his easel on deck in all weather conditions, sketching with an almost manic speed, and touring the north seas in search of icebergs with the ruthless determination of a hunter. The excitement of the chase is evoked by Noble, who describes with awe their first sighting of an iceberg: 'Enthroned on the deep in lonely majesty, the dread of mariners, and the wonder of the traveller, it was one of those imperial creations of nature that awakens powerful emotions, and illumines the imagination.'

Church's strenuous efforts, in freezing fog, at twilight, in rocking boats, in sudden squalls, and under numerous other 'disadvantages that would have mastered a less experienced hand', would eventually be condensed into his large finished canvas of *The Icebergs*, in which an element of the sublime is heightened by the presence of a destroyed ship's mast in the foreground. With this painting Church attained what had by now become the ultimate goal of the intrepid travelling artist – to portray nature at her most strikingly unusual, and to do so with an overlay of metaphor, poetry and adventure.

James Hamilton, *Kane's Brig 'Advance' Ice-locked in Smith Sound*, engraving after Abel Kane in Elisha Kane's *Arctic Exploration*, Philadelphia, 1856. The thrills of Arctic travel romanticised for the armchair traveller.

OVERLEAF Frederic Church, *The Icebergs*, 1861; oil on canvas, Dallas Museum of Art. Far from being a purely objective rendering of an arctic scene, this is essentially a romantic comment on the insignificance of man in the face of nature.

Select Bibliography

Alazard, Jean, *L'Orient et la peinture française au XIX^c siècle*, Paris, 1930

Alexander, William, *The Costume of China*, London, 1805

Alfrey, N., and Daniels, S., *Mapping the Landscape* (exhibition catalogue), University Art Gallery, Castle Museum, Nottingham, 1990

Anon, *Description de l'Egypte . . .*, 23 vols., Paris, 1809-28

Archer, Mildred, *The Daniells in India*, Washington, 1962

Archer, Mildred, *Company Drawings in the India Office*, 2 vols., London, 1972

Archer, Mildred, *Early Views of India: The Picturesque Views of Thomas and William Daniell 1786-1794*, London, 1980

Archer, Mildred, *The India Office Collection of Paintings and Sculpture*, London, 1986

Archer, Mildred, and Bastin, John, *The Raffles Drawings in the India Office Library*, London, 1978

Archer, Mildred, and Lighbown, Ronald, *India Observed: India as Viewed by British Artists, 1760-1860*, Victoria and Albert Museum, London, 1982

Archer, Mildred, and Falk, Toby, *India Revealed: The Art and Adventures of James and William Fraser, 1801-35*, London, 1989

Baines, Thomas, *The Victoria Falls, Zambezi River, Sketched on the Spot, During the Journey of J. Chapman and T. Baines*, London, 1865

Baines, Thomas, *The Gold Regions of South-Eastern Africa . . . accompanied by Biographical sketch of the author*, London, 1872

Ballantine, James, *The Life of David Roberts*, Edinburgh, 1866

Bartlett, William, *Forty Days in the Desert, A Journey from Cairo to Mount Sinai and Petra*, London, 1840

Bayly, C. A. (ed.), *The Raj: India and the British, 1600-1947* (exhibition catalogue), National Portrait Gallery, London, 1991

Beacour, F., *La découverte de l'Egypte*, Paris, 1989

Beattie, William, *Brief Memoir of the late William Henry Bartlett*, London, 1855

Bendiner, Kenneth, *The Portrayal of the Middle East in British Painting, 1835-1860*, Columbia University, 1979

Berry-Hill, H. and S., *George Chinnery 1774-1852: Artist of the China Coast*, Leigh-on-Sea, 1963

Berry-Hill, H. and S., *Chinnery and China Coast Paintings*, Leigh-on-Sea, 1970

Bettex, Albert, *The Discovery of the World*, London, 1960

Bindis Fuller, R., *Rugendas en Chile*, 1973

Blunt, Wilfred, *The Art of Botanical Illustration*, London, 1950

Bodmer, Karl, *Maximilian's Reise in das innere Nord-America*, Cologne, 1838-41

Boerlin, Paul, *Frank Buchser 1828-1890*, Basel, 1990

Boogaart, E. van der (ed.), *Johann Maurits van Nassau-Siegen, 1604-1679, A Humanist Prince in Europe and Brazil*, The Hague, 1979

Boppé, A., *Les Peintres du Bosphore au 18e siècle*, Paris, 1911

Botting, Douglas, *Humboldt and the Cosmos*, London, 1973

Buchser, Frank, *Mein leben . . .*, Zürich-Leipzig, 1942

Carneiro, Newton, *Rugendas no Brasil*, Rio de Janeiro, 1979

Carr, D. J., *Sydney Parkinson, Artist of J. Cook's Endeavour Voyage*, Canberra, 1983

Catherwood, Frederick, *Views of Ancient Monuments in Central America . . .*, London, 1844

Catlin, George, *Letters . . . on North American Indians*, London, 1841

Catlin, George, *Life among the Indians*, New York, 1857

Catlin, George, *Last Rambles among the Indians of the Rocky Mountains and the Andes*, New York, 1867

Catlin, George, *Catalogue . . . of Catlin's Indian Cartoons*, New York, 1871

Cawley, Robert, *Unpathed Waters: Studies in the Influence of the Voyages on Elizabethan Literature*, Princeton, 1940

Chaumelin, M., *Decamps, sa vie, son oeuvre et ses imitateurs*, Paris, 1861

Clayton, Peter, *The Rediscovery of Ancient Egypt: Artists and Travellers in the 19th Century*, London, 1982

Commer, Patrick (ed.), *The Inspiration of Egypt: Its Influence on British Artists, Travellers and Designers, 1700-1900* (exhibition catalogue), Brighton Museum and Art Gallery, 1983

Cumpston, J. H. L., *Thomas Mitchell, Surveyor-General and Explorer*, Melbourne, 1954

Cunningham, Allan, *The Life of David Wilkie*, London, 1843

Daniell, T. and W., *Oriental Scenery . . .*, London, 1797

Daniell, T. and W., *A Picturesque Voyage to India by the Way of China*, London, 1810

Daniell, W., *Views in Bootan*, London, 1813

Davidson, Angus, *Edward Lear, Landscape Painter and Nonsense Poet*, London, 1938

Davillier, Baron, *Life of Fortuny*, Philadelphia, 1885

Delacroix, Eugène, *Selected Letters, 1813-63*, trans. Jean Stewart (introduction by John Russell), London, 1971

Drexel, Francis Martin, *Journal of a Trip to South America, 1826-1830*, Philadelphia, 1916

Edwards, Edward, *Anecdotes of Painting*, London, 1808

Elwes, Robert, *A Sketcher's Tour round the World*, London, 1854

Fairchild, H. N., *The Noble Savage*, New York, 1928

Field Hering, F., *Gérôme, His Life and Works*, New York, 1892

Flandin, Eugène Napoleon, *Voyage en Perse*, Paris, 1851-4

Foster, W., *British Artists in India, 1760-1820*, Walpole Society, Vol. 19, London, 1930-31

Fraser, James Baillie, *Views in the Himala Mountains*, London, 1820

Fromentin, E., *Un été dans le Sahara*, Paris, 1856

Fromentin, E., *Une année dans le Sahel*, Paris, 1857

Fromentin, E., *Voyage en Egypte (1869)*, Paris, 1935

Gonse, Louis, *E. Fromentin, Peintre et écrivain*, Paris, 1881

Goodall, Frederick, *The Reminiscences of Frederick Goodall, R.A.*, London, 1902

Goupil, F., *Voyage en Orient fait avec Horace Vernet en 1839 et 1840*, Paris, 1843

Griffiths, Anthony, and Kesnerova, Gabriela, *Wenceslas Hollar, Prints and Drawings from the collections of the National Gallery, Prague and the British Museum, London* (exhibition catalogue), London, 1982

Hackforth-Jones, J., *The Convict Artists*, South Melbourne, 1977

Hackforth-Jones, J., *Augustus Earle, Travel Artist*, Canberra, 1980

Hills, Patricia, *The American Frontier: Images and Myths* (exhibition catalogue), Whitney Museum, New York, 1973

Hodges, William, *Travels in India . . .*, London, 1793

Hommaire de Hell, X., *Voyage en Turquie et en Perse . . .*, Paris, 1854

Honour, Hugh, *Chinoiserie: The European Vision of Cathay*, London, 1961

Honour, Hugh, *The New Golden Land: European Images of America from the Discoveries to the Present Time*, New York, 1975

Honour, Hugh, *The European Vision of America* (exhibition catalogue), National Gallery, Washington, 1975-6

Hulton, Paul, and Quinn, David, *The American Drawings of John White, 1577-1590*, London, 1954

Hulton, Paul, *The Work of Jacques Lemoyne*, London, 1977

Hulton, Paul, *The Complete Drawings of John White*, London, 1984

Huntingdon, David, *Frederic Edwin Church* (exhibition catalogue), National Collection of Fine Arts, Washington, 1966

Isaacs, Revd Albert Augustus, *A Pictorial Tour in the Holy Land*, London, 1863

Joppien, R., and Smith, B., *The Art of Captain Cook's Voyages*, 3 vols., London, 1985-7

Juler, Caroline, *Les orientalistes de l'école Italienne*, Paris, 1987

Jullian, Philippe, *The Orientalists*, Oxford, 1977

Kane, Elisha Kent, *Arctic explorations*, Philadelphia, 1856

Laurens, J., *La légende des ateliers, fragments et notes d'un peintre, 1842-1900*, Carpentras, 1901

Lewis, J. M. H., *John Frederick Lewis R.A. 1805-1876*, Leigh-on-Sea, 1978

Linton, W., *The Scenery of Greece and its Islands*, London, 1856

Llewellyn, B., *The Orient Observed: Images of the Middle East from the Searight Collection*, London, 1989

Lüdeke, E., *Büchser Amerikanische Sendung*, Basel, 1941

Macaulay, Rose, *The Pleasure of Ruins*, London, 1951

Manthorne, Katherine Emma, *Tropical Renaissance, North American Artists Exploring Latin America, 1839-1879*, Washington DC, 1989

Marcos, Fouad, *Fromentin et l'Afrique*, Sherbrok, 1974

Mitchell, Thomas Livingstone, *Three Expeditions into the Interior of Eastern Australia*, London, 1838

Mitchell, Thomas Livingstone, *Journal of an Expedition into the Interior of Tropical Australia*, London, 1848

Moorehead, Alan, *Darwin and the Beagle*, London, 1969

Murphy, Ray, *Edward Lear's Indian Journal*, London, 1953

Murray-Oliver, Anthony, *Augustus Earle in New Zealand*, Christchurch, 1968

Neal Solly, N., *Memoir of the Life of W. S. Müller*, London, 1875

Niebuhr, Carsten, *Reisebeschreibung nach Arabien und andern umliegende Laendern*, Copenhagen, 1772 (English edition, London, 1792)

Noakes, Vivien, *Edward Lear, The Life of a Wanderer*, London, 1968

Noakes, Vivien, *Edward Lear, 1812-1888* (exhibition catalogue), Royal Academy of Arts, London, 1985

Noakes, Vivien, *The Painter Edward Lear*, London, 1991

Noble, Reverend Louis L., *After Icebergs with a Painter*, New York, 1861

Novak, Barbara, *Nature and Culture: American Landscape and Painting, 1825-75*, New York, 1980

Nygren, Edward J., and Robertson, Bruce (eds.), *Views and Visions: American Landscape before 1830* (exhibition catalogue), Wadsworth Atheneum, Hartford, Connecticut, 1986

Pal, P., and Dehejia, V., *From Merchants to Emperors: British Artists and India, 1757-1930*, Ithaca, 1986

Park, F., *Wanderings of a Pilgrim in Search of the Picturesque*, London, 1850

Parry, Elwood, *The Image of the Black Man in American Art*, New York, 1974

Pennington, Richard, *A Descriptive Catalogue of the Etched Work of W. Hollar 1607-77*, Cambridge, 1982

Penrose, Boies, *Travel and Discovery in the Renaissance, 1420-1620*, Cambridge, Mass., 1960

Peyrefitte, Alain, *The Collision of Two Civilizations. The British Expedition to China in 1792-4*, London, 1993

Prown, Jules David (ed.), *Discovered Lands, Invented Pasts: Transforming Visions of the American West*, London and New Haven, 1992

Raquejo, Tonia, *El palacio encantado: La Alhambra en el arte británico*, Madrid, 1989

Rugendas, Johan Moritz, *Album de trajes chilenos*, Santiago de Chile, 1973

St Clair, Alexandrine, *The Image of the Turk in Europe*, New York, 1973

Searight, Sarah, *The British in the Middle East*, London, 1969

Seddon, J. P., *Memories and Letters of the Late Thomas Seddon*, London, 1858

Shellin, Maurice, *India and the Daniells*, London, 1979

Sim, Katherine, *David Roberts, R. A. 1769-1864*, London, 1984

Sim, Katherine, *David Roberts* (catalogue of an exhibition held at the Barbican Art Gallery, London), Oxford, 1986

Sitwell, S. (with Blunt, Wilfred), *Fine Bird Books, 1700-1900*, London, 1954

Smith, Bernard, *European Vision and the South Pacific*, New Haven and London, 1985

Smith, Bernard, *Imagining the Pacific: In the Wake of Captain Cook's Voyages*, New Haven and London, 1992

Smith, Bernard, and Wheeler, Alwynne, *The Art of the First Fleet*, Oxford, 1988

Smith, Henry Nash, *Virgin Land: The American West as Symbol and Myth*, Cambridge, Mass., 1982

Stevens, Mary Anne (ed.), *The Orientalists* (exhibition catalogue), Royal Academy, London, 1984

Stuebe, Isabel, *The Life and Work of William Hodges*, New York, 1979

Sturzinger, Ursula, et al., *Charles Gleyre, ou les illusions perdues*, Zurich, 1974

Sutton, T., *The Daniells: Artists and Travellers*, London, 1954

Sweetman, J., *The Oriental Obsession: Islamic Inspiration in British and American Architecture, 1500-1920*, Cambridge, 1988

Thackeray, William, *Notes on a Journey from Cornhill to Cairo*, London, 1845

Thompson, James, *The East: Imagined, Experienced, Remembered* (exhibition catalogue), National Gallery of Ireland, Dublin, 1988

Thompson, James, and Wright, Barbara, *Les Orientalistes: Eugène Fromentin*, Paris, 1987

Thornton, Lynne, *Images de Perse, le voyage du Colonel F. Colombari à la court du Char de Perse de 1833 à 1848*, Paris, 1981

Thornton, Lynne, *Les Orientalistes, peintres voyageurs 1828-1908*, Paris, 1985

Thornton, Lynne, *Women as Portrayed in Orientalist Painting*, Paris, 1985

Torre-Revello, J., *Los artistas pintores de la expedición Malaspina*, Buenos Aires, 1944

Trench, Richard, *Arabian Travellers*, London, 1986

Tsigakou, Fani-Maria, *The Rediscovery of Greece*, London, 1981

Von Hagen, Victor Wolfgang, *Frederick Catherwood*, New York, 1950

Visiteurs de l'Empire Céleste (exhibition catalogue), Musée national des arts asiatiques Guimet, Paris, 1994

Waldeck, Frédéric de, *Voyage pittoresque et archéologique dans le province du Yucatan*, Paris, 1838

Wallis, John, *Thomas Baines of King's Lynne, Explorer and Artist*, London, 1820-75

Wyld, William, *Voyage pittoresque dans la Régence d'Alger exécuté en 1833*, Paris, 1835

Index

Illustration Acknowledgements

The Trustees of the British Museum: 6-7, 17, 18-19, 21, 22, 23, 26 (above), 27, 31, 33, 34, 38, 39, 40, 41, 43 (above and below), 50, 51, 56, 66 (above), 73, 76, 77, 79, 89, 92, 107, 110 (above and below), 111, 116 (above and below), 133. The British Library: 14, 54, 57, 58, 59, 61, 63 (above and below), 64, 66 (above), 67, 70, 71, 74 (left and right), 75, 81 (above and below), 85, 90, 91, 141, 149, 151. Akademie der bildenden Künste, Kupferstichkabinett: 8. National Maritime Museum, London: 10-11, 83 (above and below), 86-7, 98-9. The National Library of Australia: 13, 15, 100, 102-3. Fitzwilliam Museum, University of Cambridge: 26 (above). Sir Brinsley Ford CBE, Hon. FRA, FSA: 29, 30. The Houghton Library, Harvard University: 28, 52. Musée d'art et d'histoire, Genève: 35. The Tate Gallery: 46, 47. Hôtel de Ville, Bagnères-de-Bigorre: 53. P&O Steam Navigation Company, Art Collection: 2, 62. Dixson Galleries, State Library of New South Wales: 94. Muséum d'Histoire Naturelle, Le Havre: 95 (above and below). Mitchell Library, State Library of New South Wales: 96-7, 152. New York Public Library: 106. R.M.N.: 114. National Museum of Denmark, Department of Ethnography: 115, 118, 119. Beinecke Rare Book and Manuscript Library, Yale University: 117, 124. Joslyn Art Museum, Omaha, Nebraska: 120, 123. Oeffentliche Kunstsammlung, Basel, Martin Bühler: 122. The Metropolitan Museum of Art: 125-6, 138-9. Jenks Studio of Photography: 130-31. National Gallery of Art, Washington: 135. The Brooklyn Museum: 137. The Detroit Institute of Arts: 142-3. The Henry E. Huntington Library and Art Gallery: 145, 146. Hunterian Museum and Art Gallery: 147. Dallas Museum of Art: 154-5.